FOOTBALL

A HISTORY OF THE BEAUTIFUL GAME

FOOTBALL

A HISTORY OF THE BEAUTIFUL GAME

KEIR RADNEDGE

igloo

igloo

Published in 2011
by Igloo Books Ltd
Cottage Farm
Sywell
NN6 OBJ
www.igloo-books.com

M044 0311

10 9 8 7 6 5 4 3 2 1

ISBN: 978-0-85734-771-8

Printed and manufactured in China

CONTENTS

THE ORIGINS OF THE GAME

Modern football first took shape in 19th century England. The Football Association was formed in 1863 as a result of meetings to establish an agreed set of Laws of the Game. The FA introduced the world's first Cup competition in 1872. Sixteen years later, 12 clubs from the north and midlands founded the Football League—the first-ever professional league. Yet the game itself can trace a history back as far as ancient China.

THE ORIGINS
OF THE GAME

Modern football is only a century-and-a-half old, but competitive ball-kicking games can be traced back much earlier. FIFA recognizes the ancient Chinese game *tsu-chu* (or *cu-ju*) as modern football's oldest ancestor.

Tsu-chu was popularized around 200–300BC as an exercise in the army. In one variation, players kicked a feather-filled ball into a 12–16 inch (30–40cm) net hung between two 30 foot (9m) high bamboo poles. In AD600, the Japanese game *kemari* was invented. Players passed a small, grain-filled ball between themselves without letting it touch the ground.

Early versions of football in Europe came from the Greek and Roman Empires. These games were more similar to rugby than modern football, with players able to use their hands as well as their feet. The Roman version, known as *harpustum*, grew into *calcio*, a notoriously violent Renaissance game, which gives its name to modern Italian football.

MEDIEVAL FOOTBALL

Records of medieval football (called fute-ball) in France and Britain tell of violent mobs charging through towns, using anything from a pig's bladder

PAGE 6 Gabriele Bella's painting of a game of football in Venice in the 18th century

PAGE 7 Fans on their way to the 1923 FA Cup final between West Ham United and Bolton Wanderers

RIGHT A medieval game of football at the Piazza Santa Maria Novella in Italy

to the head of a defeated Danish prince as a ball. Football was so competitive, popular, and disruptive that it caused riots. Both the Lord Mayor of London in 1314 and Henry VIII in 1540 attempted to ban the sport, despite Henry having his own pair of football boots.

RULES AND REGULATIONS

By the 19th century, football—or soccer, as it was also known from its earliest years—had started to take a more recognizable shape as part of British public school curriculums. Two unofficial sets of rules, one from Cambridge University and another developed by clubs in the north east of England, were established to govern the game.

The English Football Association (FA) was formed in 1863 and published the first consolidated set of formal laws. Rebel schools, which wanted to permit running while holding the ball, abandoned association football and launched rugby football.

AN INTERNATIONAL GAME

Football quickly spread around the world as sailors, engineers, bankers, soldiers, and miners introduced it wherever they went. Clubs were formed in Copenhagen, Vienna, and Genoa, with British colonial outposts further aiding the spread of the game. In 1891, Argentina became the first nation outside the UK to establish a football league and British sailors helped to popularize the game in Brazil. Even the United States had its own "soccer" teams as far back as the 1860s. By the end of the century, leagues—albeit not necessarily national ones at this early stage— were running in England, Scotland, Italy, Holland, and pre-communist Russia.

The first international match took place the year after the inaugural FA Cup, when England played Scotland in 1872, at Hamilton Crescent, Partick, Glasgow. The British Home Internationals quickly became a fixture.

THE ORIGINS
OF THE GAME

THE CREATION OF FIFA

By the start of the 20th century, national football associations had been formed in countries across Europe and South America, including Uruguay, Chile, Paraguay, Denmark, Sweden, Italy, Germany, Holland, Belgium, and France.

Carl Anton Wilhelm Hirschman of Holland suggested convening an international meeting of football associations to the English FA's secretary, F. J. Wall. The English FA was initially positive, but left the call unanswered. Robert Guerin from the French Sports Association didn't want to wait indefinitely and, at a match between France and Belgium in 1904, he invited the European associations to join together.

This time the English FA made it clear it was not interested. However, the others agreed and FIFA (Fédération Internationale de Football Associations) came into being on 21 May 1904, in Paris, when representatives agreed a list of regulations, including playing matches according to the English Football Association's law book. Represented at the meeting were France, Belgium, Denmark, Holland, Spain, Sweden, and Switzerland.

FOOTBALL FACTS

300–200BC *tsu-chu* popularized in China
AD600 *kemari* developed by the Japanese aristocracy
12th century both women and men took part in huge games in England
1314 "football" banned by the Lord Mayor of London
1530 a famous *Calcio* game takes place during the siege of Florence
1848 "Cambridge Rules" published by Cambridge University
1863 English Football Association founded with a set of codified laws for modern football

RIGHT Crowds build at the 1923 FA Cup "White Horse Final" between West Ham United and Bolton Wanderers

The seeds were sown for the World Cup, with Article Nine stipulating that FIFA would be the only body with the authority to organize such an international tournament.

Although none of the British nations attended the founding meeting of FIFA, they joined two years later and England's D. B. Woodfall became president.

ENGLAND'S INFLUENCE

The English game remained revered around the world in those days, proof of which is to be found in the English clubs names which survive far and wide. Clubs named after Arsenal are to be found in countries as far apart as Ukraine and Argentina and the famous amateur team, the Corinthians, saw their title adopted by what is now one of Brazil's greatest clubs.

In Italy, the English legacy is still evident in the names of clubs such as Milan and Genoa—not the Italian "Milano" and "Genova"—while the fervent Basque supporters of Athletic Bilbao in northern Spain maintained a private insistence on "Atleti" despite the Franco dictatorship imposing the Spanish-language "Atletico" label.

Students who came to England for an education also took home with them more than the latest developments in engineering, finance, and commerce. One such was Charles Miller, whose Scottish father, a railway engineer in Sao Paulo, had sent his son "home" for an English boarding school education. Young Miller returned to Brazil in 1894 with two footballs in his baggage—and sparked a passion which resulted in a record five World Cup triumphs.

Jimmy Hogan, William Garbutt, and Arthur Pentland were outstanding among English football coaches who taught the finer points of the game on the continent in the first half of the 20th century. Hogan worked in Hungary and then in Austria whose national team he coached in their famously narrow 4-3 defeat by England at Stamford Bridge in 1932.

THE ORIGINAL LAWS OF THE GAME

(as adopted by the Football Association on December 8, 1863)

1. The maximum length of the ground shall be 200 yards, the maximum breadth shall be 100 yards, the length and breadth shall be marked off with flags; and the goal shall be defined by two upright posts, eight yards apart, without any tape or bar across them.

2. A toss for goals shall take place, and the game shall be commenced by a place kick from the center of the ground by the side losing the toss for goals; the other side shall not approach within 10 yards of the ball until it is kicked off.

3. After a goal is won, the losing side shall be entitled to kick off, and the two sides shall change goals after each goal is won.

4. A goal shall be won when the ball passes between the goal-posts or over the space between the goal-posts (at whatever height), not being thrown, knocked on, or carried.

5. When the ball is in touch, the first player who touches it shall throw it from the point on the boundary line where it left the ground in a direction at right angles with the boundary line, and the ball shall not be in play until it has touched the ground.

6. When a player has kicked the ball, any one of the same side who is nearer to the opponent's goal line is out of play, and may not touch the ball himself, nor in any way whatever prevent any other player from doing so, until he is in play; but no player is out of play when the ball is kicked off from behind the goal line.

7. In case the ball goes behind the goal line, if a player on the side to whom the goal belongs first touches the ball, one of his side shall be entitled to a free kick from the goal line at the point opposite the place where the ball shall be touched. If a player of the opposite side first touches the ball, one of his side shall be entitled to a free kick at the goal only from a point 15 yards outside the goal line, opposite the place where the ball is touched, the opposing side standing within their goal line until he has had his kick.

8. If a player makes a fair catch, he shall be entitled to a free kick, providing he claims it by making a mark with his heel at once; and in order to take such kick he may go back as far as he pleases, and no player on the opposite side shall advance beyond his mark until he has kicked.

9. No player shall run with the ball.

10. Neither tripping nor hacking shall be allowed, and no player shall use his hands to hold or push his adversary.

11. A player shall not be allowed to throw the ball or pass it to another with his hands.

12. No player shall be allowed to take the ball from the ground with his hands under any pretence whatever while it is in play.

13. No player shall be allowed to wear projecting nails, iron plates, or gutta-percha on the soles or heels of his boots.

THE WORLD CUP

The World Cup is the planet's greatest sports event.
In terms of competing nations, television viewers,
and finance, it dwarfs every other tournament.
Uruguay were the first hosts—and first winners—in
1930, but the worldwide game is perfectly balanced:
South American nations have won nine cups and so
have Europe's finest. Brazil have carried off the golden
trophies a record five times, followed by Italy (four)
and Germany (three).

THE WORLD CUP
FOUNDATION & 1930s

After a string of false starts, the World Cup was launched in 1930. The inaugural international tournament was the British Home Championship, but FIFA's first attempt to launch a truly international championship in 1906 had fallen flat. Switzerland agreed to host the tournament and even made a trophy, but no-one turned up.

PAGE 12 Italy score the first goal in the 1982 World Cup final

PAGE 13 Italy's Fabio Cannavaro lifts the 2006 trophy

THE RESULT 1930

Location: Montevideo
Final: Uruguay 4 Argentina 2
Shirts: Uruguay white, Argentina light blue-and-white stripes
Scorers: Dorado, Cea, Iriarte, Castro; Peucelle, Stabile

URUGUAY
Ballesteros
Nasazzi   Mascheroni
Andrade Fernandez Gestido
Dorado Scarone Castro Cea Iriarte
M Evaristo Ferreira Stabile Varallo Peucelle
Suarez   Monti   J Evaristo
Paternoster   Della Torre
Botasso
ARGENTINA

England, now a member of FIFA, organized the first large-scale international football tournament as part of the 1908 London Olympic Games.

FIFA became a genuinely international body as countries from North and South America started to join. The Olympic football tournament continued, and from 1914 FIFA took a lead role, officially designating it the "world championship of amateur football."

Yet FIFA still harbored ambitions of launching its own tournament. Not only was the status of football in the Olympics insecure—it was almost dropped entirely from the 1932 Games at Los Angeles—but interest was hampered by the sudden spread of professionalism.

URUGUAY WIN ON HOME TERRITORY
In the 1920s, two Frenchmen, FIFA President Jules Rimet and French Federation Secretary Henri Delaunay, set up a steering committee. In 1928, the FIFA Congress in Amsterdam voted to support a first world championship and Uruguay's bid to host the event easily beat off European

RIGHT Czech goalkeeper Planicka punches clear in the 1934 final

competition. As part of the country's centenary celebrations, the event was guaranteed financially by the government. The Uruguayans boasted an impressive pedigree as double Olympic champions—in 1924 they won in France and four years later they triumphed in Amsterdam—and built the massive Centenario Stadium in Montevideo.

Lucien Laurent of France scored the first-ever World Cup goal in the 4-1 victory over Mexico, but Uruguay's generosity in hosting the tournament was rewarded with ultimate victory, when 80,000 fans packed the Centenario Stadium to witness their 4-2 win over Argentina in the final.

WORLD CUP 1934

Italy were both hosts and winners of the first finals to be staged in Europe. Dictator Benito Mussolini wanted to put on a show to impress his international visitors. But World Cup title holders Uruguay stayed away because they feared their top players would remain in Europe.

Vittorio Pozzo, Italy's manager, included three Argentinian-born players in his squad, while his best home-grown players were forwards Giuseppe Meazza and veteran Angelo Schiavio.

Spain became Italy's most awkward opponents. The heroics of the legendary Spanish goalkeeper Ricardo Zamora held the hosts to a 1-1 draw in the quarter-finals. However, Zamora took such a battering from Italy's over-physical forwards that he was not fit enough to play in the replay.

Italy won 1-0 and then defeated Austria, Europe's other top nation, by the same score. In the final they beat Czechoslovakia 2-1, but only after extra time, with Schiavio scoring the winner.

ABOVE Leonidas (left) leads Brazil to their victory over Sweden in 1938

WORLD CUP 1938

Four years later, Italy won a second time, this time in France. The atmosphere was very different compared to 1934, when Pozzo's team had benefited from home advantage, generous referees, and home support. In France they were jeered by fans angered by Italy's fascist politics.

England, despite being outside FIFA, were invited to compete at the last minute in place of Austria—which had been swallowed up by Adolf Hitler's Germany. However, England's Football Association declined the invitation, even though they had thrashed Germany 6-3 in Berlin shortly before the finals.

The favorites included Brazil, following their astonishing first round match against Poland. Brazil won 6-5 in extra time: Brazil's Leonidas and Poland's Ernst Wilimowski both scored hat-tricks.

Brazil were so confident of beating Italy in the semi-finals that they rested Leonidas to keep him fresh for the final, but their gamble misfired because they lost 2-1. Italy went on to defeat Hungary 4-2 in the final to become the first-ever back-to-back World Cup winners.

THE WORLD CUP
1950s

"All I remember was everyone in tears."

PELÉ RECALLS THE 1950 FINAL

A nation was traumatized when the host, and one of the favorites, Brazil lost to Uruguay in the climax of the first postwar World Cup. The competition ended not with a one-off final but a four-team group, a format not used since

1950

The closing match, in front of a record crowd of nearly 200,000 in Rio's Maracana Stadium, proved decisive as Uruguay claimed their second title.

Free-scoring Brazil needed only a draw to win their first World Cup, and looked to be on their way when Friaça fired them into the lead. But underdogs Uruguay, captained and marshaled by center half Obdulio Varela, stunned the hosts with late goals by Juan Schiaffino and Alcides Ghiggia. Brazilian fans were furious with their team's failure, with much of the blame heaped on unfortunate goalkeeper Barbosa.

The defeat marked the very last time that Brazil wore an all-white uniform, which was believed to be so unlucky that it was replaced by the now famous yellow shirts. Because of the result, the Uruguay players remained in their dressing room for hours after the final whistle until it was safe to emerge.

The final was not the only shock of the tournament—England had been humbled in the first round by the United States. England lost 1-0 at Belo Horizonte, courtesy of a goal from Haiti-born Joe Gaetjens.

1954

When runaway favorites Hungary thrashed under-strength West Germany 8-3 in their opening round group game, no one expected these sides to meet again in the final—let alone for the West Germans to triumph.

RIGHT 1954 souvenir postcard featuring the Maracana Stadium and views over Rio de Janerio

THE RESULT 1950

Location: Rio
Final: Uruguay 2 Brazil 1
Shirts: Uruguay light blue, Brazil white
Scorers: Schiaffino, Ghiggia; Friaça

URUGUAY

Máspoli

Gambetta   Gonzáles

Andrade   Varela   Tejera

Ghiggia Julio Pérez Miguez Schiaffino Morán

Chico   Jair   Ademir   Zizinho   Friaça

Danilo   Bauer   Bigode

Juvenal   Augusto

Barbosa

BRAZIL

West Germany's coach Sepp Herberger rested several key players for their first game, while Hungary's captain Ferenc Puskás suffered an ankle injury that was meant to rule him out of the rest of the tournament. Yet Puskás, as the star player, was controversially brought back for the final and even gave his Magical Magyars a sixth-minute lead. Left winger Zoltan Czibor scored again almost immediately, with another rout looking likely.

But the Germans made a spirited comeback. Led by captain Fritz Walter and two-goal hero Helmut Rahn, the Germans battled back for what is known in footballing history as "Das Wunder von Bern"—the miracle of Berne.

Hungary entered the tournament as Olympic champions and overwhelming favorites, but remarkably the final would be their only defeat between 1950 and early 1956.

They thought they had done enough to take the match into extra time, only for an 88th-minute Puskás strike to be controversially disallowed for offside by Welsh linesman Mervyn Griffiths.

The competition produced an amazing 140 goals over 26 matches, including the World Cup's highest-scoring match during Austria's thrilling 7-5 triumph over Switzerland.

1958

Brazil finally ended their wait for their first World Cup crown, with a little help from their latest superstar, Pelé, in Sweden. The 17-year-old Santos prodigy had to wait until Brazil's final group game to make Vicente Feola's starting line-up, with mesmerizing winger Garrincha also given his first opportunity at the finals.

The pair proved irresistible by setting up Vavá for both goals to beat the Soviet Union, before Pelé grabbed a hat-trick in the 5-2 semi-final success over France. Brazil defeated hosts Sweden by the same score in the final, including two goals by Pelé, who broke down in tears at the end.

Yet Brazil were not the only ones to impress. French striker Just Fontaine scored 13 goals, a record for a single World Cup tournament that no one has since come close to emulating. The 1958 finals were also the only time that all four of the UK's Home Nations qualified, although England had lost Duncan Edwards and several other international players in the Munich air disaster.

West Germany lost a bitter and violent semi-final to Sweden. Captain Fritz Walter was fouled out of the game and could not be replaced because substitutes were not allowed at the time.

BELOW Brazil's 17-year-old Pelé shoots for goal in the 1958 final

THE RESULT 1954

Location: Berne
Final: West Germany 3 Hungary 2
Shirts: West Germany white, Hungary cherry red
Scorers: Morlock, Rahn 2; Puskás, Czibor

WEST GERMANY

Turek

Posipal   Liebrich   Kohlmeyer

Eckel   Mai

Rahn   Morlock   O Walter   F Walter   Schäefer

Tóth   Puskás   Hidegkuti   Kocsis   Czibor

Zakarias   Bozsik

Lantos   Lantos   Buzánszki

Grosics

HUNGARY

THE RESULT 1958

Location: Stockholm
Final: Brazil 5 Sweden 2
Shirts: Brazil blue, Sweden yellow
Scorers: Vavá 2, Pelé 2, Zagallo; Liedholm, Simonsson

BRAZIL

Gilmar

D Santos   Bellini   Orlando   N Santos

Zito   Didi

Garrincha   Vavá   Pelé   Zagallo

Skoglund   Liedholm   Simonsson   Gren   Hamrin

Parling   Börjesson

Bergmark   Gustavsson   Axbom

Svensson

SWEDEN

Pelé (far right) raises his arms in celebration after scoring Brazil's fifth goal in the 1958 World Cup final against Sweden

THE WORLD CUP
1960s

Even without Pelé at the helm, Brazil were unstoppable as they comfortably retained their title in South America. Pelé scored in Brazil's first game but was injured in the next match, so he played no further part in the tournament.

RIGHT Garrincha (left) and Amarildo celebrate Brazil's equalizer against Czechoslovakia in the 1962 final

THE RESULT 1962
Location: Santiago
Final: Brazil 3 Czechoslovakia 1
Shirts: Brazil yellow, Czechoslovakia red
Scorers: Amarildo, Zito, Vavá; Masopust

BRAZIL

Gilmar

D Santos   Mauro   Zozimo   N Santos

Zito   Didi   Zagallo

Garrincha   Vavá   Amarildo

Jelinek   Kvasnak   Scherer   Pospichal

Masopust   Kadraba

Novák   Popluhár   Pluskal   Tichy

Schroif

CZECHOSLOVAKIA

1962

Pelé's deputy was Amarildo from Botafogo of Rio de Janeiro. Known as "the white Pelé," he made an immediate impact by scoring two goals in the 2-1 win over Spain in their decisive concluding group match. Amarildo also notched an equalizer in the final, but the undisputed star of the tournament was Garrincha, nicknamed "the Little Bird." Garrincha, the world's greatest-ever dribbler, was the two-goal man of the match as Brazil saw off England 3-1. He even overcame the embarrassment of being sent off in the 4-2 semi-final win over hosts Chile.

Brazil managed to persuade the disciplinary panel not to ban their star player, so he played in the final. The defending champions suffered an early shock when midfielder Josef Masopust shot the Czechoslovakians into an early lead. However,

mistakes by goalkeeper Vilem Schroif helped Brazil hit back to register a 3-1 victory. Masopust's consolation, months later, was to be voted as the European Footballer of the Year.

Chile's preparations had been marred by an earthquake two years earlier, yet they surpassed expectations not only off the pitch but on it as they clinched a deserved third place.

The Chileans caused a quarter-final upset by knocking out the highly rated Soviet Union, despite the outstanding efforts of legendary goalkeeper Lev Yashin.

1966

A historic hat-trick hero, a Soviet linesman, and a dog named Pickles were all made famous by the World Cup hosted in England.

West Ham's Geoff Hurst, who started the finals as a reserve striker, became the only man ever to score three goals in a World Cup final as the hosts beat West Germany 4-2 at Wembley Stadium.

But his second strike was one of the most controversial in football history. West Germany leveled through Wolfgang Weber's 89th-minute goal to take the final into extra time. In the first-half of extra time, Hurst produced an angled shot that struck the underside of the crossbar and went down behind the goal line before bouncing back out again for the Germans to clear it to safety.

England claimed they had scored and, despite West Germany's protests, linesman Tofik

Bakhramov told Swiss referee Gottfried Dienst that the ball had indeed crossed the line.

Hurst, who fell while shooting at goal, was unsighted. However, fellow striker Roger Hunt was so certain that the ball had crossed the line that he did not bother even following up to put it back into the net. The controversial goal left the Germans deflated and Hurst capped his performance by claiming his hat-trick—and England's greatest footballing triumph—with virtually the last kick of the contest.

Alf Ramsey's hard-working side, nicknamed the "Wingless Wonders," had edged past Uruguay, Mexico, France, Argentina, and Portugal en route to the final. However, there were some complaints that England had been able to play all their matches in their stronghold of Wembley Stadium.

Their quarter-final against Argentina proved to be the most bitter. Visiting captain Antonio Rattin was sent off for dissent by German referee Rudolf Kreitlein but initially refused to leave the pitch and eventually had to be escorted by police.

The tournament had been boycotted by African nations, who were unhappy at their "winner" having to qualify via a play-off with the champions of Asia or Oceania.

BRAZIL MISS PRESENCE OF PELE

For the second successive World Cup finals, Pelé limped out of the tournament early on after being the victim of relentlessly tough tackling. His aging team-mates were unable to raise their game without their star player, and Brazil surprisingly crashed out in the first round.

It was also a story of woe for former champions Italy, whose squad were pelted with rotten vegetables on their return home. They suffered a 1-0 defeat to the minnows of North Korea, whose winner was drilled home by dentist Pak Doo Ik. The Koreans raced into a 3-0 quarter-final lead over Portugal, before Mozambique-born Eusébio inspired the Portuguese to a 5-3 comeback and slotted home four goals.

Eusébio, dubbed the "Black Panther" for his goal scoring prowess, ended the tournament as top scorer with nine goals but was denied a place in the final by Bobby Charlton's two goals, which guided England to a 2-1 semi-final success.

Less than four months before England captain Bobby Moore accepted the Jules Rimet trophy from Queen Elizabeth II, it had been stolen from a London exhibition. Fortunately, a mongrel dog called Pickles dug up the trophy from a South London garden and was promptly rewarded with a lifetime's supply of pet food.

THE RESULT 1966

Location: London
Final: England 4 West Germany 2
Shirts: England red, West Germany white
Scorers: Hurst 3, Peters; Haller, Weber

ENGLAND

Banks

Cohen   J Charlton   Moore   Wilson

Ball   Stiles   B Charlton   Peters

Hurst   Hunt

Emmerich   Held   Seeler

Overath   Beckenbauer   Haller

Schnellinger   Weber   Schulz   Höttges

Tilkowski

WEST GERMANY

ABOVE Pickles, the dog who found the stolen World Cup

LEFT England captain Bobby Moore holds aloft the Jules Rimet trophy

The German players celebrate their equalizing goal in the second half of the 1966 World Cup final

THE WORLD CUP
1970s

This was the first World Cup to be broadcast in sun-soaked color around the world. Nothing could match Brazil's famous yellow shirts as Mario Zagallo showcased arguably the most dazzling attacking side in footballing history.

1970

Spearheaded by Pelé, JaiArzinho, Rivelino, and Tostão, Brazil were allowed to keep the Jules Rimet trophy after becoming the first country to win three World Cups. Pelé became the only player with a hat-trick of victories, although in 1962 he had been injured very early in the tournament.

Brazil featured in a classic first round contest, when they defeated England 1-0. However, both sides qualified for the quarter-finals. England's title defense came to a dramatic end when West Germany avenged their 1966 final defeat to bounce back from a two-goal deficit to register an extra time 3-2 win over Sir Alf Ramsey's men. The effort of overcoming England undermined the Germans in their semi-final against Italy, and West Germany ran out of steam and lost another epic, to be edged out 4-3.

Brazil wrapped up the tournament with a 4-1 triumph over Italy in Mexico City. Brazil's fourth goal was the finest of the tournament, and one of the most memorable ever scored in a final. A smooth passing move, the length of the pitch, was finished off by captain Carlos Alberto. Manager Mario Zagallo became the first man to win the World Cup both as a player and a manager.

THE RESULT 1970
Location: Mexico
Final: Brazil 4 Italy 1
Shirts: Brazil yellow, Italy blue
Scorers: Pelé, Gerson, Jairzinho, Carlos Alberto; Boninsegna

BRAZIL

Felix

Alberto Brito Piazza Everaldo

Clodoaldo Gerson Rivelino

Jairzinho Tostao Pelé

Riva Boninsegna
(Rivera)

De Sisti Mazzola Bertini Domenghini
(Juliano)

Facchetti Rosato Cera Burgnich

Albertosi

ITALY

RIGHT Jairzinho scores Brazil's third goal against Italy

1974

Franz Beckenbauer achieved the first half of his own leadership double when he captained hosts West Germany to victory over Holland. The final was played in Munich's Olympic Stadium, the footballing home to Beckenbauer and his FC Bayern team-mates—goalkeeper Sepp Maier, defenders Hans-Georg Schwarzenbeck and Paul Breitner, and strikers Uli Hoeness and Gerd Müller.

Yet the dominant personality of the finals was Holland's center forward Johan Cruyff who, as captain, epitomized their revolutionary style of total football, characterized by a high-speed interchange of playing positions.

Hosts West Germany surprisingly stuttered in the first round but managed to qualify despite suffering a shock defeat to East Germany, who had emerged through the Berlin Wall for the first and last time in World Cup history. Jürgen Sparwasser made a name for himself with an historic strike in the 77th-minute to secure a slender 1-0 success.

West Germany topped their second round group ahead of Poland—qualifying victors over England—while Holland topped the other group ahead of an over-physical Brazil.

English referee Jack Taylor awarded the first World Cup final penalty—Cruyff had been fouled in the opening minute at Munich. Johan Neeskens stepped up to put the Dutch ahead before the hosts had even touched the ball.

West Germany soon leveled matters through a penalty kick and went ahead decisively, courtesy of Müller, just before the half-time interval.

1978

Holland had to settle for second best again, this time without the inspirational Cruyff, who refused to travel to Argentina, amid kidnap fears.

Cruyff's absence was particularly missed in the final as the hosts clinched their inaugural World Cup 3-1 after extra time. Argentina's only European-based player, Mario Kempes, finished as top scorer, with six goals, including two goals in the final.

A ticker-tape assisted storm of home support carried manager César Menotti's Argentina through the first round and to the second group with a tricky meeting against Peru. Needing to win by at least four clear goals, Menotti's men ran out contentious 6-0 winners to deny Brazil a final berth. Instead, Brazil settled for a 2-1 win over Italy in the third place play-off.

In the final, Holland went behind to a Kempes strike before half-time and equalized through substitute striker Dick Nanninga. On the verge of the full-time whistle, Rob Rensenbrink's effort was denied by the post and proved a costly miss as Argentina pulled away in extra time with further goals from Kempes and Daniel Bertoni.

Scotland failed to progress beyond the first round and were shamed by Willie Johnston being kicked out of the tournament after failing a dope test. The dazzling left winger protested his innocence, insisting he was taking Reactivan tablets to treat a cold, but he was banned from internationals and his playing career fizzled out.

LEFT Holland's Johan Cruyff holds off a West German defender

Johan Neeskens (left) fires the ball home from the penalty spot to score the first goal of the 1974 World Cup final

1938   1958   1966

ABOVE Just Fontaine parades his top-scoring golden boot

RIGHT France striker Fontaine on the way to his record 13 goals

ABOVE Portugal's Eusébio is floored for a penalty against North Korea

BELOW Geoff Hurst rises above the West German defense at Wembley

ABOVE Czech forward Jan Riha ouwits Brazil's Domingos da Guia

1970

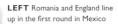

LEFT Romania and England line up in the first round in Mexico

BELOW Brazil's Jairzinho is sent flying by a Uruguayan defender

ABOVE England left back Terry Cooper outwits West German captain Uwe Seeler

LEFT Weary England await extra time in their quarter-final in Leon

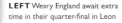

1974

ABOVE Top-scoring Gerd Müller eludes Yugoslav keeper Enver Maric

BELOW Franz Beckenbauer (white) breaks up a Dutch attack

THE WORLD CUP
1980s

The competition swelled to 24 sides in 1982, as Spain played hosts for the first time. Italy ended a 44-year wait for their third title, with captain Dino Zoff becoming the oldest player to win a World Cup at the grand age of 40.

1982

Toni Schumacher, West Germany's goalkeeper, was fortunate to have been playing in the final. Despite having knocked unconscious France's Patrick Battiston with a brutal foul during a thrilling semi-final in Seville, he somehow escaped punishment.

In the final, Schumacher faced a spot kick from Antonio Cabrini and the Italian left back made history by becoming the first player to miss a penalty in the title decider. In the same match, German Paul Breitner wrote himself into the annals of history when he became the first player to score a penalty in two separate finals.

But second half goals from Paolo Rossi, Marco Tardelli, and Alessandro Altobelli handed Enzo Bearzot's attacking side the trophy. Rossi's hat-trick in a 3-2 win had earlier knocked out a Brazil team that included Falcao, Socrates, and Zico.

Rossi finished up as the tournament's six-goal leading marksman to claim the Golden Boot. This was an astonishing achievement because the Juventus striker had returned to top-class football only six weeks earlier, following a two-year suspension for his role in a match-fixing scandal.

Holders Argentina struggled from the outset and they introduced their new hero, 21-year-old Diego Maradona, who had narrowly missed out on a place in their previous World Cup squad. Yet Maradona was stifled in the opening match, beaten 1-0 by Belgium, and then sent off for retaliation during a second round defeat by Brazil.

Spain were one of the more disappointing World Cup hosts out on the pitch, sensationally beaten by Northern Ireland in their opening match and later eliminated after finishing bottom of a three-nation second round group behind West Germany and England.

A further change of format saw the knockout

RIGHT Claudio Gentile and skipper Dino Zoff celebrate in Madrid

semi-finals restored. Italy defeated Poland 2-0 in Barcelona to make the final, then West Germany saw off France in Seville, courtesy of the first penalty shoot-out in World Cup history. A magical match swung one way, then the other: Germany opened the scoring but trailed 3-1 before battling back with two goals to force extra time. Schumacher went from villain to hero by stopping the crucial last French penalty from Maxime Bossis.

1986

After his previous World Cup disgrace, Maradona jumped into the spotlight when, virtually single-handedly, he won Argentina their second World Cup by combining audacious skills with equally audacious law-breaking.

The world saw the best and worst of Maradona in a five-minute spell of Argentina's quarter-final contest against England. Although the Argentinian captain punched the ball into the back of the net, Tunisian referee Ali bin Nasser allowed the goal to stand (this was his first and last World Cup game as a referee).

Maradona claimed the goal was "a little bit of Maradona, a little bit of the hand of God," a boast that accompanied him for years to the delight of a nation that considered the trick a belated answer to Argentina's military and naval defeat by Britain in the 1982 Falkland Islands conflict.

However, no one could dispute the majesty of Maradona's second strike. A solo slalom took him the full length of the England half, before he swept the ball past embattled goalkeeper Peter Shilton with his left foot, for one of the best-ever goals. Just to prove this had been no accident, maverick Maradona scored a similar solo goal in the 2-0 semi-final victory over Belgium.

Despite being closely marked by West Germany's Lothar Matthäus in the final, Maradona escaped long enough to provide the defense-splitting pass that set up Jorge Burruchaga's late goal to once more clinch World Cup success. The Germans had clawed their way back from a two-goal deficit and looked to be heading toward

extra time, before the glittering run and pass from match-winner Maradona.

Franz Beckenbauer, a World Cup winner with West Germany in 1974, was in charge of the national team. Yet even his magic touch off the pitch was simply no match for the genius of Maradona on it.

England's consolation was that striker Gary Lineker went on to win the Golden Boot as the tournament's leading scorer with six goals. His tally included a hat-trick in England's first round defeat of Poland, which sent them to the quarter-finals against Paraguay. England had struggled initially, losing their opening game 1-0 to Portugal, and in the scoreless draw against Morocco they lost key players—Ray Wilkins was sent off and captain Bryan Robson was helped off with an injury.

European champions France sneaked past Brazil on penalties in their quarter-final, but for the second successive World Cup fell in the semi-final to West Germany. The Germans simply cruised into the final against Argentina, courtesy of goals from Andreas Brehme and Rudi Völler.

BELOW Diego Maradona sends Peter Shilton the wrong way

THE WORLD CUP
1990

"It was simple: we worked hard and we deserved it."

GERMANY'S LOTHAR MATTHÄUS

West Germany overcame Diego Maradona and Argentina, gaining revenge for their 1986 final defeat, which meant Franz Beckenbauer joined Brazil's Mario Zagallo as the only other man to win a World Cup as player and coach.

Victory in the Stadio Olimpico saw history made as Franz Beckenbauer became the first man to have won separate World Cups as coach and captain (Zagallo had not captained Brazil), while Argentina saw red and paid the penalty for their negative tactics in the final. Beckenbauer stepped down after the triumphant return home and was promptly succeeded by his former assistant Berti Vogts. However, the Germans have not won a World Cup since.

Unlike four years earlier, the final showdown of Italia '90 was a dull defensive game. Settled by Andreas Brehme's controversial late penalty, it was marred by red cards for Argentina's Pedro Monzon and Gustavo Dezotti. This was the first time that a player had been sent off in a World Cup final.

The 1990 finals were later considered as one of the poorest tournaments in the event's history, partly because of the inferior quality of refereeing. Sepp Blatter, then the general secretary of world governing body FIFA and later its president, decided then and there to launch a campaign to improve refereeing standards.

CAMEROON BRING AN AFRICAN BEAT

Argentina were not a patch on the team who had won the World Cup for the second time in their history just four years earlier. Inspirational captain Diego Maradona was carrying a knee injury and in their showpiece opening match they were pulled apart by nine-man Cameroon, the African surprise

package. The Africans, making their debut in the World Cup finals, beat the holders 1-0, thanks to a historic strike from François Omam Biyik.

Cameroon's secret weapon was veteran striker Roger Milla. He provided some of the tournament's highlights but Cameroon were let down by their indiscipline. The Africans led England, managed by Bobby Robson, 2-1 in their quarter-final contest in Naples, but slack defending opened up gaps, which prompted them into conceding two penalties. Both were converted by Gary Lineker, who helped drive England through to their first semi-final appearance for 24 years.

But England's fortune with penalties ran out when they faced West Germany. England finished 1-1 after extra time, but lost the penalty shoot-out 4-3 after Stuart Pearce and Chris Waddle missed their spot-kicks.

England, managed for the last time by Robson, who was moving to PSV Eindhoven, lost to hosts Italy in the third place play-off. By then, the Tottenham midfielder Paul Gascoigne had become a national icon, both for his performances as well as for the tears he shed after being shown a yellow card in the semi-final defeat by the Germans. The card was Gascoigne's second of the tournament, which meant he would have missed the final had England reached that grand stage. Later, Gascoigne returned to Italy to play for Lazio.

England were not the only nation to suffer the pain of penalty punishment. In the second round,

THE RESULT 1990

Location: Rome
Final: West Germany 1 Argentina 0
Shirts: West Germany white, Argentina blue
Scorers: Brehme (pen)
Sent Off: Monzón, Dezotti

Romania fell in the shoot-out to the Irish Republic, who were making an impressive debut under manager Jack Charlton, and Argentina edged past both Yugoslavia in the quarter-finals and hosts Italy in the last four through penalty kicks.

The finest match in the tournament was arguably the second round duel between old rivals Holland and West Germany. Tension surrounding the game was exacerbated in the first half by the expulsions of Holland midfielder Frank Rijkaard and German striker Rudi Völler. Ultimately, West Germany won 2-1, thanks to a sensational performance by striker Jürgen Klinsmann—possibly the best of his career—who scored and made the other goal.

Argentina's new hero, especially in the shoot-outs, was goalkeeper Sergio Goycochea. The first choice, Nery Pumpido, was injured in Argentina's opening group game against the former Soviet Union, so Goycochea played instead.

MARADONA AT HOME IN NAPLES

The duel between Italy and Argentina was staged in Naples, where Maradona was plying his trade at club level. His appeal for Napoli fans to cheer for Argentina backfired, yet they still won.

The downside for Argentina was that their outstanding winger, Claudio Caniggia, received a yellow card for a second time in the tournament and so was suspended from playing in the final.

Maradona had played remarkably throughout Italia '90, considering his injury. But in the final his luck ran out, and he pointed the blame at everyone except himself, including FIFA's Brazilian president João Havelange.

The final straw for Maradona was the controversial award of a late penalty to West Germany for a foul on striker Völler. Lothar Matthäus was the designated German penalty taker. But, citing a muscle strain, the captain handed over the responsibility to Brehme, who made no mistake in shooting past Goycochea.

ABOVE Andy Brehme celebrates his World Cup-winning penalty against Argentina

THE WORLD CUP
1994

After missing out to Mexico in 1986, the United States finally hosted a World Cup and proved better than expected on the pitch by reaching the second round before bowing out to the eventual champions—Brazil.

The Americans had set themselves a goal of staging the event back in the late 1960s. They had failed with a bid to host the finals in 1986, but won FIFA approval through both their commercial potential and a promise to build a solid professional league.

Bora Milutinovic, a freelance Yugoslav coach, was hired to build a national team on the strength of his work in guiding Mexico, as hosts, to the quarter-finals in 1986. His "Team America" reached the second round before narrowly losing to Brazil, the eventual winners.

The finals proved surprisingly successful, with the average attendance for the tournament reaching its highest-ever figure of 69,000. The total attendance of 3.6 million became the then highest attendance in World Cup history.

The tournament was also the most attended single sport sporting event in US history, and featured the first-ever indoor match in the World Cup finals, when the US hosted Switzerland in the Pontiac Silverdome in Michigan, Detroit.

The competition kicked off at Soldier Field Stadium in Chicago with another penalty miss, when veteran pop star Diana Ross rolled a pretend spot-kick wide during a glitzy opening ceremony in front of US President Bill Clinton.

The opening match saw holders Germany edge past Bolivia 1-0, courtesy of Jürgen Klinsmann's strike on the hour mark. Ultimately, the Germans, playing for the first time as a unified team since the collapse of the Berlin Wall, were dethroned 2-1 by Bulgaria in the quarter-finals.

One of the favorites to win overall had been Colombia, led by their maverick frizzy-haired playmaker Carlos Valderrama, who was dubbed "El Pibe"—the kid. The Colombians had been tipped for great things by no less a judge than Pelé, after an incredible 5-0 win away to Argentina during the qualifying competition, in which winger Faustino Asprilla exploded onto the international scene. Unfortunately, their campaign proved both short-lived and tragic. They failed to progress beyond the

THE RESULT 1994

Location: Los Angeles
Final: Brazil 0 Italy 0 (after extra time; Brazil 3-2 on penalties)
Shirts: Brazil yellow, Italy blue

BRAZIL

Taffarel

Jorginho   Aldair   Márcio Santos   Branco
(Cafu)

Mazinho II   Dunga   Mauro Silva   Zinho
(Paulo Viola)

Romário   Bebeto

R Baggio   Massaro

D Baggio   Albertini   Berti   Donadoni
(Evani)

Maldini   Baresi   Mussi   Benarrivo
(Apolloni)

Pagliuca

ITALY

first group stage, when central defender Andrés Escobar scored an own goal in their 2-1 defeat by the United States.

Colombia's squad returned home to a furious reception from fans and media. The furore was cut short within days, after Escobar was shot dead after an argument near his home. His killer was later jailed for 43 years, but served only 11 years of the sentence before being paroled.

MARADONA MAKES HASTY EXIT

Diego Maradona's final World Cup also proved controversial and short-lived. In 1991 he had fled Italy in disgrace after failing a dope test for cocaine and was banned for 15 months while playing for Napoli. He made a comeback in Spain and then Argentina, playing his way back into the national squad in time for the World Cup finals.

However, after scoring and starring in an opening win against World Cup newcomers Greece, Maradona then failed a further dope test for the stimulant ephedrine, following Argentina's 2-1 win over Nigeria, and was immediately expelled from the tournament. Maradona later blamed the dope test failure on the weight-loss drugs he had been taking prior to the World Cup finals.

His shocked team-mates were not long in following him home to Buenos Aires after their unexpected 3-2 exit at the hands of Romania in the last 16 knockout stage. The Romanian side was built around the creative midfield talents of Gheorghe Hagi, known as the "Maradona of the Carpathians."

For the first time since the four British Home Nations returned to the FIFA fold after World War II, none of them qualified for the finals. However, the Republic of Ireland—largely built around English league players—emerged impressively from a first round group that featured Italy, Mexico, and Norway. They fell at the next hurdle, soundly beaten 2-0 in the last 16 by Holland at the Citrus Bowl Stadium in the midday humidity of Orlando, Florida.

BRAZILIAN BLEND FAITH AND FLAIR

Brazil, despite lacking the flair of some of their previous sides, boasted the most effective strike partnership of the tournament in the European-based pair of Bebeto and Romario.

But a disappointing final against Italy ended scoreless, making it the first in the history of the World Cup to be settled by a penalty shoot-out.

The decisive kick was missed by Italian forward Roberto Baggio, whose goals had been crucial in taking his country all the way to the final at the Rose Bowl Stadium in Los Angeles, California.

Mario Zagallo, the assistant manager of Brazil to Carlos Alberto Parreira, became the first man to be involved in four World Cup winning teams, 20 years after his first attempt at gaining this distinction. Zagallo had been an invaluable outside left in Brazil's victorious teams at Sweden in 1958 and four years later in Chile. He successfully managed Brazil in 1970, but four years later his side crashed out to finish fourth.

WORLD CUP **MOMENTS**

ABOVE Keeper Jan Jongbloed comes to Holland's rescue

RIGHT Dutch defender Ruud Krol foils Scotland's Asa Hartford

BELOW Argentina's fans hail Daniel Passarella

ABOVE Diego Maradona celebrates victory over England

BELOW Gary Lineker in action against Argentina

1990

1994

ABOVE Andy Brehme converts Germany's penalty winner in the final

ABOVE Brazilian captain Dunga holds up the World Cup while he celebrates with his team-mates

LEFT Roberto Baggio despairs after missing his penalty to hand Brazil victory in the final

BELOW Romario celebrates a quarter-final goal against Holland

BELOW David Platt celebrates his winning goal in the England v Italy 3rd place playoff

THE WORLD CUP
1998

Zinedine Zidane's distinctive balding head won France their first World Cup. The midfielder's headed goals, either side of half-time, was overshadowed by a Brazilian side subdued by striker Ronaldo's pre-match collapse.

THE RESULT 1998

Location: Paris
Final: France 3 Brazil 0
Shirts: France blue, Brazil yellow
Scorers: Zidane 2, Petit
Sent Off: Desailly

FRANCE

Barthez

Thuram Leboeuf Desailly Lizarazu

Petit Deschamps Karembeu Zidane
(Boghossian)

Djorkaeff
(Vieira)

Guivarc'h
(Dugarry)

Ronaldo Bebeto

Leonardo Rivaldo Dunga César Sampaio
(Denilson) (Edmundo)

Carlos Baiano Aldair Cafu

Taffarel

BRAZIL

Internazionale striker Ronaldo had been a member of the 1994 Brazil squad, but did not play a game. Yet, by 1998 he was the team's key player and goal scorer. But crucially, on the morning of the World Cup final, he collapsed in the hotel room that he shared with Roberto Carlos, and was taken to hospital for an emergency check-up.

Manager Mario Zagallo, not expecting Ronaldo to be available to play, named an official line-up that featured Edmundo in Ronaldo's place. Surprisingly, Ronaldo appeared in the line-up after being given the medical all clear. Zagallo swiftly obtained FIFA clearance to alter the team line-up and later denied that he had been pressured into including Ronaldo by FIFA officials and/or sponsors. Although Ronaldo did play the entire match, he was never a force in the game and rarely threatened to add to his personal tally of four goals scored during the previous rounds.

Zidane's double and a last-minute third goal from midfielder Emmanuel Petit provided France with a comfortable victory in Saint-Denis, north of Paris. The 3-0 triumph was astonishing because the French side were reduced to ten men after defender Marcel Desailly was sent off.

Desailly's red card cost Thierry Henry an opportunity to make an appearance in the final. The striker had played in all the previous games and as a substitute was expected to play a part. But manager Aimé Jacquet opted to bring on a replacement defender for Desailly instead.

ABOVE Referee Kim Milton Nielsen sends off England's David Beckham

An earlier red card, in England's second round loss to Argentina, had already made David Beckham notorious. England had reached the finals by qualifying from a tough group that included Italy. Under the management of former international midfielder Glenn Hoddle, England had beaten Tunisia and Colombia in their first round group but finished in second spot because of a 2-1 reversal to Romania. It proved a costly slip up because it meant England had to tackle old rivals Argentina in the second round instead of Croatia.

England's Michael Owen, the outstanding new Liverpool striker, scored a superb solo goal, but early in the second half Manchester United midfielder Beckham was sent off by Danish referee Kim Morten Nielsen for flicking a retaliatory foot at the Argentinian midfielder Diego Simeone. England, without the influential Beckham, fought bravely and even had a potential winning "goal" by defender Sol Campbell contentiously disallowed before they eventually succumbed in the lottery of a penalty shoot-out.

Argentina's midfielder Ariel Ortega was given his marching orders during their next game against Holland. Being reduced to ten men meant the same ultimate outcome of defeat. Holland progressed to the finals with a 2-1 win, courtesy of a superb winning goal from Arsenal striker Dennis Bergkamp—later voted the best goal of the finals.

FRANCE FIND WINNING FORMULA

Dutch luck finally ran out. In their semi-final they lost on a penalty shoot-out to Brazil while hosts France, gathering speed and confidence, sneaked past Croatia thanks to the first and second goals of defender Lilian Thuram's international career. France won despite finishing with ten men after Laurent Blanc was sent off after a tussle with Slaven Bilic.

Croatia went on to finish third on their debut at the finals, less than a decade after the country had gained independence out of the wreckage of the former Yugoslavia. Star striker Davor Suker ended up as the tournament's six-goal leading marksman to crown a remarkable season and win the coveted Golden Boot. Less than two months earlier, Suker had became a European club champion with Real Madrid following their slender 1-0 victory over Juventus in the Champions League final.

France went on to defeat Brazil and duly celebrate the triumph for which they had been waiting since fellow countryman Jules Rimet had launched the inaugural World Cup 68 years earlier.

Thousands of delirious fans poured into central Paris to celebrate, and the victorious team undertook an open-top bus parade the following day down the Champs-Elysées. Manager Aimé Jacquet, a former international midfielder, was delighted with the manner of victory because he had been subjected to a barrage of relentless criticism for his tactics and team selection by the daily sports newspaper L'Equipe.

Jacquet stepped down after the finals and handed over to assistant Roger Lemerre. The new manager proved that the World Cup triumph had been no fluke by leading France to a further international victory at the subsequent European Championships two years later with a 2-1 success over Italy.

BELOW Team-mates join Zinedine Zidane in celebrating his second goal against Brazil

THE WORLD CUP
2002

"We proved the World Cup belongs to everyone."

JAPAN'S HIDETOSHI NAKATA

Although the trophy went to hot favorites Brazil, the tournament was full of upsets. Holders France made a swift exit, while co-hosts South Korea stunned Portugal, Italy, and Spain to reach the semi-finals.

RIGHT Park Ji-sung of South Korea enjoys that winning feeling against Portugal

South Korea were beaten to third place by Turkey, who had previously never progressed beyond the first round.

This was the first World Cup to be played in Asia. Japan had long been campaigning for the right to stage the finals, and one major step in their bid to impress the world authority FIFA had been the launch of the professional J.League in 1993.

Less than two years before the hosting decision, in 1996, the Japanese were challenged in the bidding race by neighbors South Korea. A major political battle within FIFA ended with a compromise that resulted in both countries being awarded the finals jointly. This decision meant that not only was the 2002 event the inaugural Asian finals but the first, and so far the only, World Cup finals to be co-hosted.

The co-hosting proved highly expensive for FIFA and highly complex in logistical terms. The match schedule for the finals had to be especially organized to ensure that each co-host played all matches in their country. In the end, the tournament organization ran remarkably smoothly.

FRANCE FAIL TO SCORE A GOAL

Out on the pitch, the first of many shocks kicked off with the tournament's grand opening match. Defending champions France were narrowly beaten 1-0 by Senegal, who were making their

debut in the finals. Midfielder Papa Bouba Diop scored the goal for the impressive and organized Senegal side.

France may have been reigning world and European champions but, in a disastrous defense of their World Cup, they were knocked out in the first round without even scoring a goal in their three group games. It was the worst record of any defending nation in the tournament's history, although they were handicapped by the initial absence of Zinedine Zidane. The key midfielder had been injured in a warm-up friendly against South Korea on the eve of the finals. Manager Roger Lemerre, who had guided France, or "Les Bleus," to victory in the European Championship two years earlier, was fired on France's return home, despite having been awarded a contract extension before the finals.

The once-mighty Argentina also failed to make the second round, after finishing third in their group behind England and table-topping Sweden.

THE RESULT 2002

Location: Yokohama
Final: Brazil 2 Germany 0
Scorers: Ronaldo 2
Shirts: Brazil yellow, Germany white

BRAZIL

Marcos

Cafu   Lúcio   Roque Júnior   R Carlos

Ronaldinho   Edmilson   Silva   Kléberson
(Paulista)

Ronaldo   Rivaldo
(Denilson)

Klose   Neuville
(Bierhoff)

Bode   Hamann   Jeremies   Schneider
(Ziege)   (Asamoah)

Metzelder   Ramelow   Linke   Frings

Kahn

GERMANY

With memories of the 1998 World Cup penalty shoot-out still fresh in their memories, Argentina tackled England indoors at Tokyo's Sapporo Dome. England emerged as 1-0 winners courtesy of a penalty converted by David Beckham, who avenged his 1998 World Cup expulsion against the South Americans.

England were guided by Swede Sven-Göran Eriksson, their first foreign manager, and beat Denmark surprisingly easily 3-0 in the second round but then lost 2-1 to Brazil in the quarter-finals. The decisive goal was a long-range fluke shot from Ronaldinho that drifted over the head of helpless England keeper David Seaman. Ronaldinho was sent off in the 57th minute, but Brazil held onto their lead without the influential midfielder for both the rest of this contest and for their semi-final 1-0 victory over Turkey.

SEMI-FINAL SLOTS FILLED BY UNDERDOGS

Japan reached the second round before being eliminated 1-0 by Turkey, while South Korea made the most of their fervent home support to race into the semi-finals and finish fourth overall. South Korea were astutely organized by the Dutch coach Guus Hiddink and inspired by attacking players such as Ahn Jung Hwan, whose extra time

goal beat Italy in a dramatic second round tie. Turkey had rarely appeared before in the finals of any major tournament, let alone the World Cup. But they made the most of this opportunity by reaching the semi-final stage. Veteran striker Hakan Sükür scored the fastest-ever goal in the World Cup by taking just 10.8 seconds to give Turkey the lead in a 3-2 win over South Korea in the third place play-off.

The final, played at the International Stadium Yokohama in Japan, belonged to Brazil's prolific striker Ronaldo. He scored twice against a competitive but uninspired German team that clearly missed their key midfielder Michael Ballack, who was suspended after collecting a second yellow card of the tournament in the semi-final.

Ronaldo finished the tournament as its eight-goal leading marksman to not only pick up the Golden Boot but to equal Pelé's Brazilian record of 12 goals overall in World Cup finals.

Oliver Kahn, Germany's captain, became the first goalkeeper to be voted as the best player of the tournament despite making a crucial error to concede the first goal in the final.

Cafu, Brazil's captain, also made history by becoming the first footballer to play in the final of three consecutive World Cups.

BELOW David Seaman is fooled by Ronaldinho's long shot

BELOW Ronaldo scores Brazil's first goal after a mistake by goalkeeper Oliver Kahn

Ronaldo (right) curls the ball around Gerald Asamoah (center) to beat German keeper Oliver Kahn (left) and score his second goal in the 2002 World Cup final

THE WORLD CUP
2006

Italy collected their fourth World Cup, although the final shall always be associated with Zinedine Zidane's violent act. The French master was aiming for a fairytale ending to his illustrious career, but instead bowed out disgracefully.

The final pitched France against Italy in Berlin's Olympic Stadium and saw Real Madrid midfielder Zinedine Zidane give France the lead with a cheeky penalty, in what was to be his final game before retiring from the sport.

Italy equalized through a header from rugged central defender Marco Materazzi, which sent the game into extra time. With ten minutes of extra time and the contest still at stalemate, Zidane suddenly launched his head into Materazzi's chest and was sent off for violent conduct by the Argentinian referee Horacio Elizondo.

Subdued France had no Zidane to help them in the penalty shoot-out. Italy, coached by Marcello Lippi, became the second side to win the World Cup on penalties after the French striker David Trezeguet hit the bar with his attempt.

Despite such a disgraceful end to his career, Zidane was voted player of the tournament because of his efforts in masterminding victories over Spain, Brazil, and Portugal to reach the final.

Italy proved to be the tournament's most consistent team, largely thanks to the contributions of the outstanding goalkeeper Gianluigi Buffon, center back and captain Fabio Cannavaro, and influential midfielder Andrea Pirlo.

Their success was all the more dramatic since it occurred at the same time as a trial in Italy, in which senior figures in club football were being accused and found guilty of systematic match-fixing. Juventus official, Luciano Moggi, was the controversial central figure in the corruption scandal. Five of Italy's successful squad and seven other World Cup players returned to Italy after the tournament to find that their club had been relegated to Serie B as punishment. The once mighty trio of Juventus, Lazio, and Fiorentina were demoted.

Italy had beaten Germany 2-0 during extra time at the semi-final stage. The hosts had been one of the most exciting teams to watch under the guidance of former striker Jürgen Klinsmann.

KLINSMANN LEADS GERMAN REVIVAL

The German federation had appointed Klinsmann, a World Cup winner in 1990, as coach in the summer of 2004, following their nation's disappointing showing at the UEFA European Championship. Klinsmann demanded a free hand, which included the right to continue to live in California and bring in his choice of new staff—coaches, assistants, and fitness experts. His approach drew initial skepticism among other coaches and fans. By the time the World Cup finals started, it became clear that Klinsmann was winning fans with his tactics and approach to matches.

Germany made an adventurous—and, crucially, winning—start, by defeating Costa Rica 4-2 in the opening game. New heroes included young striker Lukas Podolski and defender Philipp Lahm. Ultimately, the German effort was halted in a semi-final in Dortmund by Italy in what was arguably

THE RESULT 2006

Location: Berlin
Final: Italy I France I (after extra time, Italy 5-3 penalties)
Shirts: Italy blue, France white
Scorers: Materazzi; Zidane (pen)
Sent Off: Zidane

ITALY

Buffon

Grosso Cannavaro Materazzi Zambrotta

Camoranesi Gattuso Pirlo Perrotta
(Del Piero) (De Rossi)

Totti Toni
(Iaquinta)

Henry Zidane
(Wiltord)

Malouda Vieira Makélélé Ribéry
(Diarra) (Trezeguet)

Abidal Gallas Thuram Sagnol

Barthez

FRANCE

the finest game of the tournament. Italy snatched victory through last-gasp goals in extra time from Fabio Grosso and Alessandro Del Piero.

The Germans scored a 3-1 third place play-off win over Portugal, resulting in a far better finish to their campaign than many home fans had feared.

DULL ENGLAND SUFFER ON SPOT-KICKS

In contrast to the Germans, England's World Cup performances were dreary, in Sven-Göran Eriksson's third and last tournament as national coach. The quarter-finals were once again the end of the road as England lost on penalties for the second time in three World Cups, beaten by Portugal in a shoot-out for the second time in a row—after a similar finish in the 2004 UEFA European Championship held in Portugal.

England's hopes had been hindered by a pre-tournament foot injury to star striker Wayne Rooney, which delayed his arrival. Then fellow striker Michael Owen was seriously injured during a freak accident in a group game against Sweden.

Rooney was sent off for stamping on defender Ricardo Carvalho during the quarter-final contest. Cristiano Ronaldo, Rooney's Manchester United team-mate, endured a hate campaign on his return to English football after having been caught smiling and winking at the Portuguese bench following Rooney's expulsion.

Portugal's progress was ended by France, who inflicted a 1-0 semi-final defeat in a lackluster match through Zidane's 33rd-minute penalty.

South America's challenge ended in the quarter-finals. In the group stage, a surprisingly adventurous Argentina had contributed the goal of the tournament against Serbia & Montenegro, a 24-pass move finished by Esteban Cambiasso. But they lost to Germany on penalties in the quarter-finals while Brazil lost their hold on the trophy at the same stage by a 1-0 reversal to France.

German striker Miroslav Klose finished top scorer with five goals, the lowest tally since 1962, for the winner of the Golden Boot.

BELOW Italy's Marco Materazzi acclaims his equalizer in the final

BOTTOM Zinedine Zidane beats Gigi Buffon to open the score for France

THE WORLD CUP
2010

European champions Spain proved themselves the best team on the planet by adding the 2010 World Cup to their achievement when the finals were staged in Africa for the first time. Andres Iniesta's goal four minutes from the end of extra time ended rugged Dutch resistance in Soccer City, Johannesburg.

Spain were obviously the most gifted footballing side at the finals. They stood out, along with top scorers Germany, in a tournament dominated by negative tactics which spoiled too many matches.

FIFA could feel vindicated by its bold choice of South Africa as hosts. The South Africans created a carnival atmosphere and pre-tournament fears about crime proved groundless.

Yet FIFA president Sepp Blatter was so concerned by the lack of excitement on the pitch that later he set up Task Force 2014 to suggest ways of encouraging positive play at the next finals in Brazil.

Spain were more cautious than expected, though their Euro 2008 winners formed the core of the team. Xavi Hernandez and Iniesta once more bossed games fluently with their one-touch passing. But though, two years earlier, striker Fernando Torres had been in top form, this time he was hampered throughout by knee trouble. Coach Vicente Del Bosque thus used a five man midfield behind top scorer David Villa. Xavi Alonso and Sergio Busquets played anchor roles, with Pedro breaking to support Villa.

Del Bosque and his squad kept their nerve after a surprise 1-0 opening game defeat by Switzerland, when Iker Casillas made a rare mistake. Villa's goals sank Honduras, and Villa and Iniesta clinched

qualification with a 2-1 win over Chile. Spain then won each of their four knock-out games 1-0. Their total of eight goals was the lowest by any World Cup-winning side. They were also the first nation ever to win a World Cup after losing their first game.

Casillas was named Goalkeeper of the Tournament and showed why with two decisive saves from Arjen Robben in the final; Carles Puyol—who headed the semi-final winner against Germany—was an inspiring center back; Xavi and Iniesta epitomized perpetual movement; and Villa always threatened up front.

Holland were a mixture of the good and the ugly. Playmaker Wesley Sneijder scored five goals, led a victorious quarter-final rally against Brazil and shone in the semi-final victory over Uruguay. Robben was the most dangerous dribbler in the finals but he fell over at the merest touch. Midfield hard men Mark van Bommel and Nigel De Jong represented Holland's less pleasant side, frequently fouling opponents to break up play. Both were lucky to escape red cards in the final—De Jong especially for a chest high "challenge" on Xavi Alonso. So the Dutch received little sympathy outside their homeland after Iniesta swept home Cesc Fabregas's pass for the winner.

THE RESULT 2010

Location: Johannesburg
Final: Spain 1 Holland 0 (after extra time)
Shirts: Spain red, Holland orange
Scorer: Iniesta

Germany's young team netted 16 goals and finished third. They beat Argentina 4-0 and England 4-1 to reach the semi-finals. Thomas Muller won the Golden Boot for his five goals plus three assists (Villa, Sneijder, and Uruguay's Diego Forlan also scored five goals apiece). Muller was named Young Player of the Tournament. Midfielders Mesut Ozil and Sami Khedira impressed so much, both earned moves to Real Madrid.

Uruguay supplied the Player of the Tournament in skipper and striker Forlan as manager Oscar Tabarez's side surprised even themselves by reaching the semi-finals.

Unlucky Ghana came within a bar's width of becoming Africa's first semi-finalists. They were level 1-1 with Uruguay in the dying seconds of extra time in the quarter-finals when Luis Suarez handled Dominic Adiyiah's header on the line. Suarez was sent off but Asamoah Gyan fired the penalty against the bar—and Uruguay won the shoot-out 4-2.

Joint favorites Brazil were a major disappointment. Coach Carlos Dunga's controversial deployment of two defensive midfielders—Felipe Melo and Gilberto Silva—upset Brazilian critics. It also failed to halt Holland's quarter-final comeback, and Melo was sent off for stamping on Robben.

England, much fancied before the finals, disappointed too. Coach Fabio Capello failed to adapt to tournament conditions and his star, Wayne Rooney, was way below his best. In the second round match, England could claim misfortune when Frank Lampard's shot clearly crossed the line for an "equalizer" which was missed by the referee with the score 2-1 to Germany. But defensive errors let them down in the second half.

Argentina, under Diego Maradona's eccentric regime, lacked tactical sense and wasted their attacking flair. Lionel Messi, their 2009 World Player of the Year, often looked a peripheral figure.

The biggest surprise was the departure of 2006 winners Italy and runners-up France at the group stage. Italy's ageing squad went home to derision after a shock 3-2 defeat by Slovakia in their last group game. France were eliminated after defeats by Mexico and South Africa and with the players feuding openly with coach Raymond Domenech and their own federation.

The hosts left the competition elated despite their group stage exit. First half goals by Bongani Khumalo and Katlego Mphela set up victory over the French in Bloemfontein. But it was Spain, and Iniesta, who will be remembered the most.

ABOVE Uruguay's Diego Forlan (right) and Ghana's John Mensah (left) battle for the ball in a quarter-final match

BELOW The Spanish players celebrate their victory in the final

Andres Iniesta (center) wheels away in delight after
scoring the winning goal in the 2010 World Cup final

1998

2002

WORLD CUP **MOMENTS**

ABOVE Dennis Bergkamp scores for Holland past Carlos Roa of Argentina

BELOW France's Zinedine Zidane scores the first goal of the final

ABOVE Brazil's Cafu (left) and Oliver Neuville of Germany (right) battle for the ball during the final

LEFT A near miss for Hakan Sukur of Turkey during the semi-final

BELOW David Beckham scores England's winner against Argentina

2006

2010

ABOVE Nigel de Jong of Holland kicks Xabi Alonso of Spain in the chest, earning a yellow card in the final

BELOW Argentina's coach Diego Maradona celebrates a goal

ABOVE Zinedine Zidane makes an exit after being sent off

BELOW Gianluigi Buffon (right) of Italy and Fabien Barthez (left) of France prior to the penalty shoot out during the final

ABOVE Germany's Miroslav Klose (center) shields the ball from Argentina's Carlos Tevez (left) and Gabriel Heinze (right) during the quarter-final match

EUROPEAN CHAMPIONSHIP

The creation of the European Championship and
UEFA, the governing body of football in Europe,
went hand in hand. FIFA had existed since 1904
and it ruled the world, but half a century later the
European countries opted to register their own
identity. By the end of the 1950s, not only was the
European Championship a reality but the European
Champion Clubs' Cup had sparked a revolution.

EUROPEAN CHAMPIONSHIP
FOUNDATION & 1960s

The idea of a rival competition to the World Cup was nothing new. Frenchman Henri Delaunay, who lent his name to the tournament, discussed the concept before World War II but never saw his dream become reality.

PAGE 52 Miroslav Klose scores for Germany against Turkey, 2008

PAGE 53 Euro 2004 winners Greece celebrate

THE RESULT 1960
Location: Paris
Final: Soviet Union 2 Yugoslavia 1
(after extra time)
Shirts: Soviets red, Yugoslavia blue
Scorers: Metreveli, Ponedelnik; Galic

SOVIET UNION

Yashin

Tchekeli   Maslenkin   Kroutikov

Voinov   Netto

Metreveli   Ivanov   Ponedelnik   Bubukin   Meshki

Kostic   Galic   Jerkovic   Matus   Sekularac

Perusic   Zanetic

Jusufi   Miladinovic   Durkovic

Vidinic

YUGOSLAVIA

FIFA feared such a tournament for the elite might undermine the status of its own World Cup but finally, in 1958, the European Championship took shape under its original name of the European Nations Cup. Sadly, Delaunay, Secretary General of the French Football Federation, died in 1954 and was unable to witness the creation of his dream. So his colleagues ensured that his name lived on by giving the tournament the alternative title of Coupe Henri Delaunay.

The inaugural competition comprised 17 countries playing on a two-leg knockout basis followed by the semi-finals, a third place play-off and then the final in one host country—appropriately enough in France.

Spain withdrew from their quarter-final against the Soviet Union because of political pressure by dictator Francisco Franco while England, Italy and West Germany failed to enter for fear of fixture congestion. The Soviets, inspired by legendary goalkeeper Lev Yashin, went on to become the first winners. They recovered from a one-goal deficit to overcome Yugoslavia 2-1 in a tense final in the old Parc des Princes in Paris.

The next competition, in 1964, was also marred by political interference. This time, Greece withdrew, after being told to face Albania in an early round though the nations were officially at war.

At least by now Cold War tension between the Soviet Union and Spain had eased, which was

fortunate because the Soviets qualified for the finals that were hosted by Spain. In the semi-finals, the Soviet Union defeated Denmark 3-0 in Barcelona, while Spain scrambled past Hungary, courtesy of a 2-1 in extra time win in Madrid.

Spain soon went a goal behind in the final at Real Madrid's Santiago Bernabéu Stadium, much to the distress of most of the 79,115 spectators. Fortunately for the hosts, Barcelona's Jesus María Pereda equalized and Zaragoza's Marcelino Martínez wrote himself into Spanish sporting history by heading in a late winner. England had entered for the first time, but had not progressed beyond the first round. New manager Alf Ramsey saw his men held 1-1 by France at Sheffield Wednesday's Hillsborough stadium, to then collapse 5-2 four months later in Paris.

CHALLENGE OF COMPETITION CHANGES
The tournament's name was now altered to the European Championship for the 1968 event and along with it came a change of format. For this event, eight groups of teams faced each other twice, with the top nation from each group progressing to two-legged quarter finals. Italy were hosts and for the first and only time a match was decided on the toss of a coin.

England, as the reigning World Champions, qualified for the inaugural European Championship finals with largely the same squad that had won

the 1966 World Cup. So hopes were high that the Three Lions could roar to a second successive major championship. But England fell 1-0 to a late goal by Yugoslavia in
a match littered with fouls and marred by Alan Mullery's sending-off one minute from the final whistle with Dragan Dzajic scoring the decisive strike.

Italy beat the Soviets in the other semi-final on an infamous coin toss after a scoreless stalemate and no time to organize a replay.

Yugoslavia dominated in the final at Rome, but were punished for not being able to beat Dino Zoff more than once. Italy equalized nine minutes from time, made five changes for the replay and strolled past the exhausted Yugoslavs 2-0.

RIGHT The Henri Delaunay Cup

BELOW Spain vs USSR in the 1964 final, Madrid

THE RESULT 1964
Location: Madrid
Final: Spain 2 Soviet Union 1
Shirts: Spain blue; Soviets red
Scorers: Pereda, Martinez; Khusainov

SPAIN

Iribar
Rivilla   Zoco   Olivella   Calleja
Pereda   Fuste   Suarez
Amaro   Martinez   Lapetra
Khusainov   Ponedelnik   Chislenko
Korneev   Ivanov   Voronin
Mudrik   Anichkine   Shesternev   Chustikov
Yashin

SOVIET UNION

THE RESULT 1968
Location: Rome
Final: Italy 1 Yugoslavia 1 (after extra time)
Shirts: Italy blue, Yugoslavia white
Scorers: Domenghini; Dzajic

ITALY

Zoff
Burgnich   Castano   Guarneri   Facchetti
Domenghini   Ferrini   Juliano   Lodetti
Anastasi   Prati
Dzajic   Musemic   Petkovic
Holcer   Acimovic   Trivic
Damjanovic   Paunovic   Pavlovic   Fazlagic
Pantelic

YUGOSLAVIA

EUROPEAN CHAMPIONSHIP
1970s

"I don't think we could have played any better."

HELMUT SCHÖN

West Germany produced the finest football yet seen in the competition en route to a 1972 victory in Belgium, seeing off the Soviet Union at the Heysel Stadium. But both Italy and England failed to reach the finals.

THE RESULT 1972

Location: Brussels
Final: West Germany 3 Soviet Union 0
Shirts: Germany white, Soviets red
Scorers: Müller 2, Wimmer

WEST GERMANY

Maier

Höttges Beckenbauer Schwarzenbeck Breitner

Hoeness Wimmer Netzer Heynckes

Müller Kremers

Kozinkevich Banishchevsky Baidachny
(Onishenko)

Konkov Kolotov Troshkine
(Dolmatov)

Kaplichny Istomine Khurtsilava Dzodzuaschvili

Rudakov

SOVIET UNION

RIGHT Captains Bobby Moore of England and Franz Beckenbauer of West Germany, 1972

1972

Belgium had delighted their fans by sending home holders Italy along the way, while England were ousted by the in-form West Germans in the two-leg knock-out quarter-finals.

West German manager Helmut Schön rebuilt his team after reaching the 1970 World Cup semi-finals in Mexico. Veteran striker Uwe Seeler had retired, so Schön looked to fast-rising Bayern Munich for the foundation of his new team.

The key man was Franz Beckenbauer, already a World Cup hero in 1966 and 1970, who was moved back from midfield to his personally favored role of attacking sweeper.

Striker Gerd Müller was another of the 1970 heroes alongside the new stars from Bayern Munich, namely attacking left back Paul Breitner and striker Uli Hoeness. Furthermore, Schön replaced Wolfgang Overath in midfield with the Borussia Mönchengladbach playmaker general Gunter Netzer.

Beckenbauer and Netzer commanded the first leg of the quarter-final at England's Wembley Stadium guiding the Germans to their inaugural victory with a 3-1 success. They had little difficulty securing a scoreless draw in the return leg against Sir Alf Ramsey's surprisingly unadventurous England side in West Berlin.

Belgium hosted the four-team finals but faced favorites West Germany at the semi-final stage. The

Germans edged through 2-1 with two goals from the prolific Müller. In the other semi-final, the Soviet Union maintained their record of reaching the last four of every final since the tournament's inception and overcame Hungary—which missed a late penalty—via Anatoli Konkov's deflected shot.

In the final, West Germany were in control, with the Soviets psychologically beaten by their recent 4-1 thrashing at the hands of West Germany. Müller, who had scored all four in the recent friendly, was on fire in the final and notched a goal in each half in the 3-0 triumph. Midfielder Herbert Wimmer added the third to claim Germany's first European Championship in front of 50,000 fans.

1976

The tournament, in Yugoslavia, was the last in which the hosts were chosen at a late stage after the qualifying rounds. The finals went on to be expanded to eight nations, with the hosts granted automatic exemption for the qualifying rounds.

Czechoslovakia emerged as surprise winners—launching their outsiders' campaign in the semi-finals by stunning Holland. Two years earlier, the Dutch had come close to being crowned world champions and, with many of their outstanding players peaking, had been expected to reach the final at the very least.

It was a sad occasion for Johan Cruyff because it was to be his last shot at glory as an international player. This became his final major tournament in a Dutch national team shirt.

West Germany, as World Cup holders, had good reason to assume that they were well-placed to win, but that complacency meant they found themselves trailing 2-0 at halftime against hosts Yugoslavia. Gerd Müller had retired from national team football but another Müller, Köln center forward Dieter, (no relation), came to the Germans' rescue on his international debut. He scored twice in the second half with his 82nd-minute equalizer forcing extra-time. Müller went on to complete a hat-trick in a famous 4-2 victory.

The final offered yet more drama, with Czechoslovakia taking an early two-goal lead against the West Germans. Manager Helmut Schön was kept waiting until the last minute of normal time before he could celebrate an equalizer from Bernd Holzenbein. Extra time failed to produce a winner, so penalties were necessary to decide the title for the first time in the history of the championship. West Germany's Uli Hoeness was the first to crack when he kicked the ball over keeper Ivo Viktor's bar and Czechoslovakia took the title after their midfield general Antonin Panenka kept his cool and scored with a chip past the West German keeper Sepp Maier.

THE RESULT 1976
Location: Belgrade
Final: Czechoslovakia 2 West Germany 2 (Czechoslovakia 5-3 on penalties after extra time)
Shirts: Czechs red, Germany white
Scorers: Svehlík, Dobiás; Müller, Hölzenbein

CZECHOSLOVAKIA

Viktor

Pivarnik   Ondrus   Capkovic   Gögh

Dobiás   Möder   Panenka   Masny
(Vesely)

Svehlík   Nehoda
(Jurkemik)

Hölzenbein   Müller

Hoeness   Beer   Bonhof   Wimmer
(Bongartz)   (Flohe)

Vogts Schwarzenbeck Beckenbauer Dietz

Maier

WEST GERMANY

LEFT Herbert Wimmer scores West Germany's second goal in the 1972 final against the Soviet Union

EUROPEAN CHAMPIONSHIP
1980s

UEFA responded to the fast-increasing popularity of the European Championship in 1980 by opting to widen out the qualifying potential and make the finals tournament itself more of a spectacle.

1980

This time, seven countries progressed out of a solely group-based qualifying system to contest the title in Italy along with the host nation, staging the event for the second time in four tournaments. Two groups of four were contested, the winners of each progressing directly to the final in the Stadio Olimpico in Rome.

Hosts Italy had fully expected to be there for the climax after being drawn in the easier of the two groups. The formidable West Germans, holders Czechoslovakia, and two-times World Cup runners-up Holland had all wound up in the other pool. Instead Italy scored a single goal and missed out on top spot, underdogs Belgium taking their place instead. England failed to progress beyond the group, their concentration disturbed by hooligan violence at their tie against hosts Italy in Turin.

RIGHT West Germany's Horst Hrubesch hails his last-minute winning goal

TOP RIGHT Holland's captain Ruud Gullit in triumph in 1988

1984

Michel Platini dominated the finals from start to finish, scoring a record nine goals and captaining hosts France to their first major international trophy. On his way to winning the European Player of the Year three times, Platini scored the lone winning goal against Denmark in the opening match, hat-tricks against Belgium and Yugoslavia, one against Portugal in the semis and the opener against Spain in the final.

Manager Michel Hidalgo used Platini in a free attacking role at the apex of a superbly balanced midfield featuring Luis Fernandez, Jean Tigana, and Alain Giresse. They topped their group with three wins in three games, nine goals scored and only two conceded by keeper Joel Bats.

Holders West Germany failed to progress even beyond the group stage. They finished third behind Spain and Portugal and ahead of only Romania, and sacked manager Jupp Derwall, their winning boss in 1980, on their return home.

1988

Holland landed their one and only major prize in the 1988 finals in West Germany to complete a continental double, PSV Eindhoven having carried off the European Champions' Cup only weeks earlier. As ever, the Dutch had internal problems to resolve along the way. Striker Marco Van Basten had to be persuaded to play by friend and mentor Johan Cruyff. Manager Rinus Michels left Van Basten out of the line-up for the Dutch players opening group defeat by the Soviet Union, but Van Basten started next time out against England and hit a hat-trick. England, already beaten by the Irish Republic, then lost 3-1 to the Soviets and finished bottom of the group.

Confident hosts West Germany topped the other group ahead of Italy, Spain, and Denmark, but were knocked out in the semi-finals proved the end of their road. Holland hit back from one-down to beat their hosts 2-1 in extra time and followed this up by beating an injury and suspension-weakened Soviet Union in the final. Van Basten's volleyed second goal was hailed as one of the finest of all time.

The decisive match in the other group was played out in Naples between West Germany and Holland. Playing their best football since the 1974 World Cup, West Germany seized the initiative and carved out a 3-0 lead with a hat-trick by Klaus Allofs before a Johnny Rep penalty and Rene Van de Kerkhof's long-distance effort gave Holland late but vain hope. Man of the match for the Germans was young blond midfielder Bernd Schuster.

West Germany were clear favorites to beat Belgium in the final and snatched an early lead through giant center forward Horst Hrubesch. Belgium came out fighting at the start of the second half, however, and equalized through a penalty converted by Rene Vandereycken, though the Germans claimed that sweeper Uli Stielike's foul had been committed just outside the box. In the final minutes, Hrubesch scored again, heading home a corner from another outstanding newcomer in Karl-Heinz Rummenigge.

THE RESULT 1984
Location: Paris
Final: France 2 Spain 0
Shirts: France blue, Spain red
Scorers: Platini, Bellone

FRANCE

Bats
Domergue Battiston Le Roux Bossis
(Amoros)
Tigana Fernandez Platini Giresse
Lacombe Bellone
(Genghini)
Carrasco Santillana
Casas Manrique Gomez Javier
(Sarabia)
Urquiaga Puig Redondo Camacho
(Bonillo)
Echarri
SPAIN

THE RESULT 1988
Location: Munich
Final: Holland 2 Soviet Union 0
Shirts: Holland orange, Soviet white
Scorers: Gullit, Van Basten

HOLLAND

Van Breukelen
Van Aerle Rijkaard R Koeman Van Tiggelen
Vanenburg E Koeman Wouters Muhren
Gullit Van Basten
Protassov Belanov
(Pasulko)
Mikhailichenko Zavarov Litovchenko Aleinikov
Rats Demanyenko Khidiyatulline Gotsmanov
(Baltacha)
Dassaev
SOVIET UNION

Michel Platini sends the ball around the Spanish wall to score the first goal for France in the 1984 European Championship final

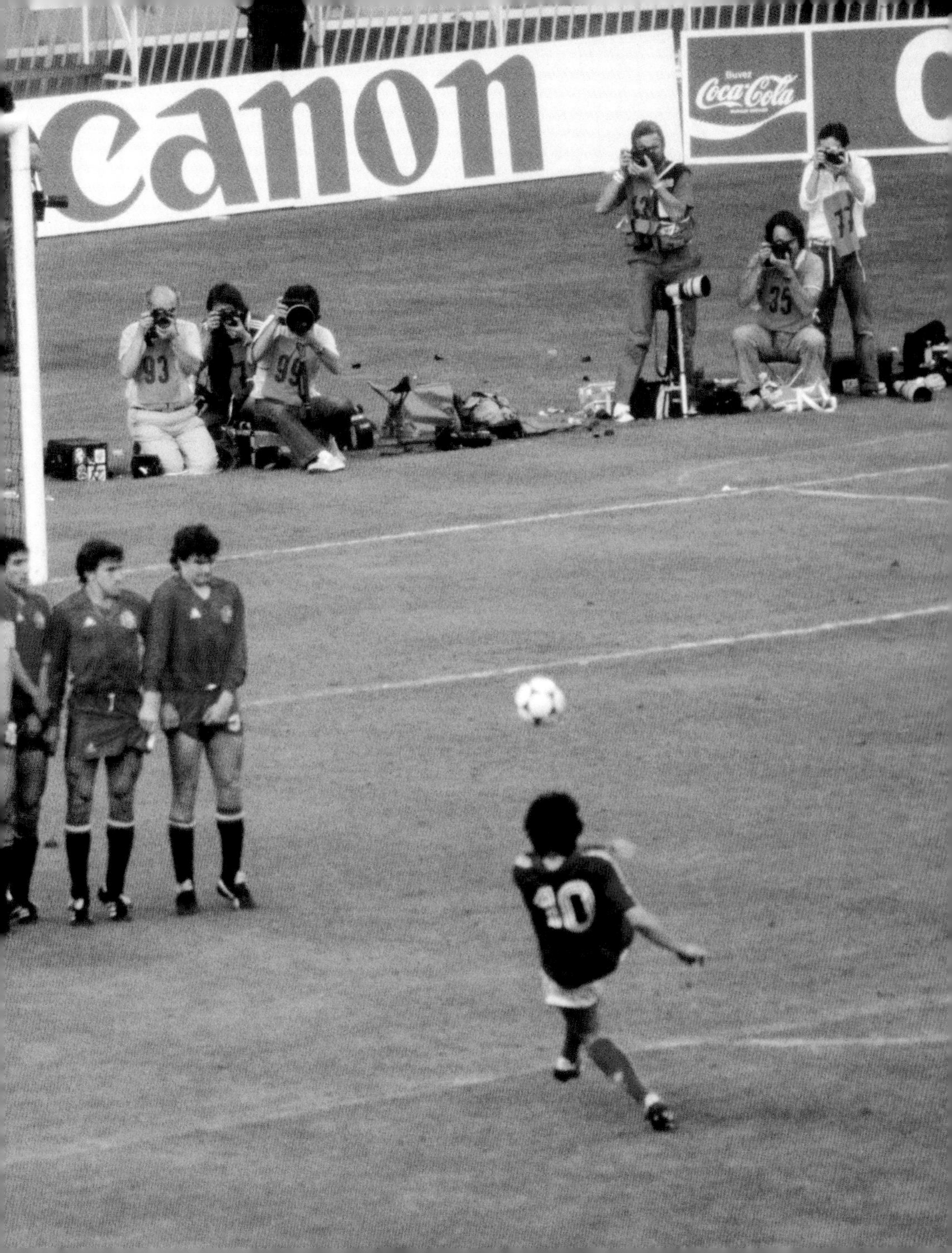
canon
Coca-Cola
93
99
35
10

1960s

1980s

LEFT Slav goal keeper Blagoje Vidinic halts a Soviet attack

BELOW England fall to hosts Italy in Turin in the first round

RIGHT Eusébio's Portugal crashed out early in the 1964 event

BELOW Michel Platini was France's nine-goal top scorer in 1984

BELOW Spain celebrate their 1964 success

1980s

1990s

2000s

BELOW Kevin Keegan is sent crashing by a Spanish defender

RIGHT Denmark's Kim Vilfort holds the 1992 trophy

BELOW Spanish reserve goalkeeper Pepe Reina (right) and teammate David Villa celebrate victory in 2008

ABOVE Iain Giresse of France controls the ball during the 1984 European Championship final

ABOVE England prepare to take the three Lions to the 2000 finals

RIGHT England celebrate their second goal against Holland in 1996

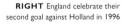

EUROPEAN CHAMPIONSHIP
1990s

The dynamic Danish team surprised Europe in Sweden in 1992. This was also the first time a unified Germany took part in international competition and the first time that players' names were printed on their backs.

1992

Denmark's remarkable feat was as unexpected as their very participation. The Danes joined the tournament only after Yugoslavia were barred for security reasons on the eve of the finals—and when the Yugoslav squad was already in Sweden—after political instability in the Balkans had erupted into armed conflict.

Richard Moller Nielsen, the Danish team's manager, was at home redecorating his kitchen when he took the call instructing him to recall his players from their family holidays in the sun.

Not surprisingly, the Danes failed initially to impress before managing to finally string their game together for the last group match against France. The French, managed by Michel Platini, disappointed despite having been unbeaten in the qualifiers and fielding an attack that featured Jean-Pierre Papin and Eric Cantona.

UEFA had changed the tournament format once more, inserting knock-out semi-finals between the group stage and the final.

Denmark, defying numerous injuries, took the lead twice in their semi-final against a complacent Holland, both goals scored by Henrik Larsen. In the resultant penalty shoot-out, Marco Van Basten—Holland's match-winner from the 1988 final—saw his penalty saved by Peter Schmeichel.

In the other semi-final, holders Germany never needed to get out of second gear on their way to a 3-2 victory over hosts Sweden. The unified German side included the likes of Karlheinz Riedle, Thomas Hässler, and Jürgen Klinsmann, and few believed Denmark could test them in the final in the Ullevi stadium in Gothenburg.

Instead, they showed skill, cunning, and determination in abundance. Schmeichel laid claim to being the best goalkeeper in the world, while Lars Olsen was a rock in the center of defense and Brian Laudrup—young brother of Michael—proved a danger on the counterattack.

Against the Germans, midfielder John Jensen put Denmark ahead and Kim Vilfort capped a fairytale fortnight with a second goal 12 minutes from the end of the game.

1996

In 1966, the number of finalists doubled to 16 for the first major tournament staged in England since the World Cup 30 years earlier. Germany clinched their third crown when Oliver Bierhoff scored the first ever "golden goal" in the competition's history.

The golden goal was a short-lived attempt to find a better solution to deciding drawn matches. Instead of using penalties, a match was halted the moment a breakthrough goal was scored during extra time.

England, who had lost in the semi-finals, at least had the satisfaction of seeing Germany, their competition, re-establish their position on the footballing map after their failure to qualify for the previous World Cup and a decade of disaster.

THE RESULT 1992
Location: Gothenburg, Germany
Final: Denmark 2 Germany 0
Shirts: Denmark red, Germany white
Scorers: Jensen, Vilfort

DENMARK

Schmeichel

Sivebaek   Nielsen   Olsen   Piechnik
(Christiansen)

Christofte   Jensen   Vilfort   Larsen

Povlsen   Laudrup

Riedle   Klinsmann

Brehme   Hässler   Sammer   Effenberg
(Doll)   (Thom)

Helmer   Reuter   Kohler   Buchwald

Illgner

GERMANY

Granting hosting rights to England had been an important signal from UEFA that it considered the English game had at last got on top of the problem of hooliganism. England boasted the finest stadia in Europe because of the massive rebuilding necessitated by the imposition of all-seater requirements.

Paul Gascoigne's wonder goal against Scotland set the tournament alight, but even better was to come when England swept Holland aside 4-1 at Wembley with a display rarely matched in their modern footballing history.

In the semi-finals, however, Germany broke English hearts by holding their nerve in a penalty shoot-out. Gareth Southgate saw his penalty saved by German keeper Andy Köpke, and midfielder Andreas Möller made no mistake with his subsequent penalty shot. The Germans thus progressed to a final back at Wembley against the technically adroit Czechs, who had ousted Aimé Jacquet's France in yet another shoot-out in the other semi-final.

The Germans, under the management of former title-winner Berti Vogts, were typically well-organized, with Matthias Sammer an excellent sweeper. But they failed initially to break down a counterattacking Czech side, who took the lead though a penalty from Patrik Berger.

The Czechs were 30 minutes from victory at that point. But then German manager Vogts sent on center forward Bierhoff as a substitute. First he equalized and then, five minutes into extra time, wrote himself into the record books with the first-ever golden goal in a major tournament.

THE RESULT 1996

Location: Wembley, London
Final: Germany 2 Czech Republic 1
(Germany on golden goal in extra time)
Shirts: Germany white, Czechs red
Scorers: Bierhoff 2; Berger

EUROPEAN CHAMPIONSHIP
2000s

France, the reigning world champions, beat Dino Zoff's Italy at the first European Championship final to be co-hosted—by Belgium and Holland—in 2000. Greece won the 2004 contest and resurgent Spain the 2008 finals.

FAR RIGHT Cristiano Ronaldo of Portugal in action during the 2004 quarter-final match between Portugal and England

RIGHT France enjoy their second title win in Rotterdam in 2000

2000

France squeezed past bitter rivals Italy in the final of the 2000 European Championship. Sylvain Wiltord equalized in the final seconds of the 90 minutes, allowing David Trezeguet to score 13 minutes into extra time with a thunderous volley. France thus became the first reigning World Cup Champions to add the European crown to their list of achievements.

Italy had come so close to winning the title, but manager Dino Zoff resigned in anger after the defeat, upset by the public criticism of his tactics and team selection by Prime Minister Silvio Berlusconi.

For England, the event proved a huge disappointment. Under the management of former player Kevin Keegan, they failed to progress beyond the group stage.

THE RESULT 2000
Location: Rotterdam
Final: France 2 Italy 1
(France on golden goal in extra time)
Shirts: France blue, Italy white
Scorers: Wiltord, Trezeguet; Delvecchio

FRANCE

Barthez

Thuram Desailly Blanc Lizarazu
(Pires)

Djorkaeff Deschamps Vieira Zidane
(Trezeguet)

Henry Dugarry
(Wiltord)

Delvecchio Totti
(Montella)

Fiore Iuliano Di Biagio Albertini
(Del Piero) (Ambrosini)

Maldini Cannavaro Nesta Pessotto

Toldo

ITALY

2004

The 2004 finals produced an upset few had predicted. Greece, who had qualified previously for only one World Cup (1994) and one European championship (1980), shocked hosts Portugal 1-0 by beating them in a dramatic final.

The Greeks, who had begun the tournament as 150-1 outsiders, also eliminated holders France as well as the Czech Republic, in this case with a silver goal, a rule that replaced the previous golden goal in 2003 before being abolished shortly afterwards. The silver goal meant that teams played on to the next formal stoppage (half-time or full-time) in extra time after a goal had been scored.

Greece's victory over Portugal in the final in Lisbon came courtesy of a solid defense, great goalkeeping, and an opportunist goal by Angelos Charisteas. The result stunned European football. However, it was not the only surprise of the tounament—Germany, Italy, and Spain had all been knocked out in the group stage.

Portugal's defeat in the final in Lisbon—in front of their own fans, denied manager Luiz Felipe Scolari a unique feat. Scolari would have become the first non-European manager to have won the continental crown.

2008

Spain ended a 44-year losing spell by winning the finals in Austria and Switzerland. Neither of the co-hosts made it through the opening group stage, but that did not affect the party atmosphere in Vienna after Spain, winners in 1964 and runners-up in 1984, defeated Germany 1-0 in the final. Liverpool's Fernando Torres scored the winning goal after 33 minutes.

Veteran manager Luis Aragones, a reserve to the winners of 1964, said afterwards: "At last we have proved that Spain can win the big prizes." After years of underachievement in major tournaments, Spain won all six of their matches, albeit they needed two fine saves from goalkeeper-captain

Iker Casillas to defeat World Cup-holders Italy on penalties in the quarter-finals. Xavi Hernandez, the Barcelona midfielder who laid on Torres's goal in the final, was hailed as UEFA's official player of the tournament.

Portugal, Croatia, Holland, and Spain were decisive winners of the groups. All were certain of qualifying after two of their three matches and rested key players in their concluding matches. That break in competitive momentum proved fatal for all but Spain, however, since the other three all lost in the quarter-finals.

Portugal blamed their quarter-final exit to Germany partly on the distractions raised by manager Luiz Felipe Scolari's imminent move to Chelsea, and partly on a media frenzy over the uncertain future of Cristiano Ronaldo.

Germany struggled to get the better of Austria in their concluding group match before defeating Portugal and then Turkey 3-2 in a dramatic semi-final. Major disappointments were World Cup runners-up France, who were first-round failures.

THE RESULT 2004

Location: Lisbon, Portugal
Final: Greece 1 Portugal 0
Shirts: Greece white, Portugal red
Scorers: Charisteas

PORTUGAL
Ricardo
Miguel   Andrade Ricardo Carvalho Nuno
(Paulo Ferreira)   Valente
Ronaldo Maniche   Costinha   Deco
         (Rui Costa)
     Figo   Pauleta
                 (Nuno Gomes)

Charisteas   Vryzas
              (Papadopoulos)
Giannakopoulos Basinas Katsouranis Zagorakis
            (Venetidis)
Fyssas   Dellas   Kapsis   Seitaridis
         Nikopolidis
GREECE

THE RESULT 2008

Location: Vienna, Austria
Final: Spain 1 Germany 0
Shirts: Spain red, Germany white
Scorers: Torres

SPAIN
Casillas
Ramos   Puyol   Marchena   Capdevila
         Senna
Iniesta Xavi Fabregas Silva
              (Alonso) (Cazorla)
         Torres
         Klose
         (Gomez)
Podolski Ballack Schweinsteiger
Hitzlsperger (Kuranyi) Frings
Lahm   Metzelder Mertesacker Friedrich
(Jansen)
         Lehmann
GERMANY

Fernando Torres of Spain (left) battles with Germany's Per Mertesacker (right) during the 2008 European Championship final

EUROPEAN CHAMPIONSHIP 2012

The European Championship is the most prestigious tournament for national teams outside the World Cup. The finals are held every four years. The next finals—in 2012—will be hosted jointly by Poland and Ukraine. The opening game will be in Warsaw on 8 June. The final will be played in Kiev on 1 July.

EUROPEAN CHAMPIONSHIP
2012

Only 17 teams entered the first championship which began in 1958. A crowd of just 18,000 in the old Parc des Princes in Paris watched the final, between the Soviet Union and Yugoslavia—and the game was screened live in only a handful of countries.

In 2010, 51 teams began the lengthy qualification competition to join joint hosts Poland and Ukraine in the finals.

European governing body UEFA expects around 1.4 million fans, from all over the world, to flood into the host nations for Euro 2012. The final will be watched by a sell-out 63,000 crowd and followed by a TV audience numbering hundreds of millions, in more than 200 countries. Worldwide

viewing figures may even exceed the 287 million who watched Spain beat Germany 1-0 in the Euro 2008 final.

Poland and Ukraine are the first nations from the old Soviet bloc to stage the finals. They are the third co-hosts, following Belgium/Holland in 2000 and Austria/Switzerland in 2008.

Their joint venture was the winner of a lengthy bidding process. There were four other

PAGE 70 Craig Levein of Scotland (left), Vicente del Bosque of Spain (2nd left), Michal Bilek of the Czech Republic (2nd right) and Aleksandrs Starkovs of Latvia (right) after the 2012 European Championship qualifying draw ceremony

PAGE 71 Mesut Ozil of Germany and Timmy Simons of Belgium vie for the ball during a qualification match

RIGHT Crowds celebrate in Poznan following the announcement that Poland and the Ukraine will co-host the 2012 European Championship

candidates—Italy, Croatia/Hungary, Turkey, and Greece.

Italy started favorites because it already had grounds and infrastructure in place. Italy had also hosted the finals in 1968 and 1980, as well as the 1938 and 1990 World Cup finals. Turkey and Greece were eliminated at the first stage.

UEFA's executive committee made its choice on 18 April 2007, after a delay to allow the remaining contenders to fine-tune their bids. Poland/Ukraine received eight votes, Italy four, Croatia/Hungary none.

A desire to break new ground by choosing eastern hosts clearly helped the Poland/Ukraine bid while Italy suffered through problems in its domestic game. A betting scandal rocked Italian football in 2006, while football-related violence led to the death of a policeman at Catania and revealed safety concerns at several stadia.

Organizing committees were set up in both countries, headed by Polish football association president Grzegorz Lato—their great forward of the 1970s—and Ukrainian association president

Grigoriy Surkis. Their slogan is "Creating History Together."

Four cities in each country were picked to stage matches—Warsaw, Gdansk, Poznan, and Wroclaw in Poland; Kiev, Lviv, Donetsk, and Kharkiv in Ukraine. Other venues were discarded—Chrozow and Krakow in Poland, Odessa and Dniprpetrovsk in Ukraine. The opening game was confirmed for the Polish capital Warsaw and the final for the Ukrainian capital Kiev.

Six new stadia are under construction, in Warsaw, Gdansk, Wroclaw, Kiev, Lviv, and Donetsk. The grounds in Poznan and Kharkiv are undergoing major renovation work.

Roads, transport facilities, hotels, and local infrastructure are being upgraded across both countries. But progress has not gone smoothly, especially in Ukraine. Work at Kiev's Olympic Stadium was held up because of problems with the roof. The main contractor was replaced after work at the New Stadium in Lviv was delayed too. UEFA president Michel Platini warned the

THE VENUES

Warsaw – National Stadium
Capacity: 53,224
Gdansk – PGE Arena
Capacity: 40,818
Poznan – Municipal Stadium
Capacity: 42,004
Wroclaw – Municipal Stadium
Capacity: 40,610
Kiev – Olympic Stadium
Capacity: 63,195
Donetsk – Donbass Arena
Capacity: 50,055
Kharkiv – Metalist Stadium
Capacity: 38,500
Lviv – New Stadium
Capacity: 30,000

EUROPEAN CHAMPIONSHIP
2012

The cost of the construction work has become a major issue in both countries. Critics claim the money could be better spent elsewhere, particularly in a time of hardship. Others, including the respective governments, view hosting the finals as a prestige project which will give a much-needed fillip to their economies and tourist industries.

Neighboring Russia is likely to bring thousands of supporters if it qualifies. But the biggest spenders will be the fans of the major western teams—Germany, Holland, and England—who always travel in big numbers to major tournaments. Tickets are due to go on sale on 1 March 2011, though most visitors will probably delay buying until the final participants are decided later that year.

The draw for the qualifying stage was made in Warsaw on 7 February 2010. The 51 teams were divided into six groups of six and three groups of five. The groups were seeded, with European champions (and World Cup holders) Spain automatic top seeds.

The top team in each, plus the best overall runner-up qualify automatically for the finals. The second teams in the other groups will be drawn in two-leg play-offs to decide the remaining four places.

In the finals, the teams are drawn in four groups of four. The top two in each contest the knock-out stage of the competition, starting with the quarter-finals. There will be 31 matches in all. The quarter-finals begin in Warsaw on 21 June, with games on each of the next three days, in Gdansk, Donetsk, and Kiev. The first semi-final will be in Donetsk on 27 June, the second clash in Warsaw the following day.

This will be the last time that 16 teams contest the finals. UEFA will increase the number of places to 24 for Euro 2016.

ABOVE The new Municipal Stadium in Poznan, under construction in 2010

organizers not to "slip behind" in their plans.

Business analysts said Ukraine faced funding difficulties because of the world economic downturn. UEFA general secretary Gianni Infantino admitted in March 2010: "We are concerned, because the problems are serious." Platini added that there were "doubts" about Ukraine's readiness.

Ukraine president Viktor Janukovich said: "I understand that we've been lagging behind the timetable and thus must take special measures to raise our building programme."

However, by August 2010, Platini said he was happy with preparations in both Poland and Ukraine and saw "no major obstacles" ahead.

Poland had faced a different problem. In September 2008, the Polish government suspended the national football association because of corruption issues. The government planned to appoint its own administrator then backed down after UEFA warned that Poland risked losing the tournament if the government interfered in football matters.

The finals were originally staged with four teams, then extended to eight in 1980. The current format took shape in 1996, when UEFA expanded the numbers to 16, to accommodate the new nations—such as Ukraine—which had emerged from the break-up of the Soviet Union and the old Yugoslavia.

Penalty shoot-outs will once more decide games level after extra time. They were introduced in 1976 (and settled the final that year). They always guarantee drama—and tears for the losers. But the law-making International Board has consigned to history the "Golden Goal" and "Silver Goal" routes to an extra time winner.

The "Golden Goal" formula (which decided the 1996 final) meant the first side to score in extra time won. The "Silver Goal"—adopted for Euro 2004—meant the team which led at the end of first half extra time won. Both schemes were considered unfair to the side which fell behind and they were discarded for Euro 2008.

A major modern tournament would be incomplete without massive sponsorship and broadcasting deals. Six worldwide brands—known as Global Partners—have signed million-dollar agreements with UEFA to sponsor the finals: adidas, Carlsberg, Castrol, Coca Cola, Hyundai-Kia, and McDonald's. All will enjoy exclusive marketing rights in their own fields, with competitors excluded from the stadia and environs.

Euro 2012 is regarded as an important international event by European governments. So most demand that matches are shown on free, terrestrial TV, not satellite subscription channels. UEFA has bowed to that pressure, but will still benefit hugely from exploiting broadcast/TV rights, with internet and mobile phone access included.

In September 2009, it sold the broadcast rights to the European Broadcasting Union (EBU) in a deal covering 36 countries. The EBU is a group of public service national broadcasters which will screen the games free to air.

Meanwhile, UEFA plans to sign individual rights agreements with terrestrial broadcasters in Europe's "big five" markets—England, Germany, France, Italy, and Spain.

The governing body has concluded deals with subscription channels outside Europe though, including the Arab network Al Jazeera Sport for the rights in North Africa and the Middle East. It is also likely to sell broadcast rights to a satellite channel for coverage in North America.

In Brazil, it has even sold the rights to two competing stations. Subscription channel Sport TV will screen all 31 games live, while the Globo network will show 23 free to air live games plus highlights packages.

So Euro 2012 is poised to net UEFA another financial bonanza. The 2008 finals in Austria and Switzerland produced a profit of $394 million (£240 m) for the governing body.

Holders and world champions Spain entered the qualifiers as favorites to retain their title. Most of their double-winning stars will still be available in 2012. Germany's young team, which reached the 2010 World Cup semi-finals, appeared obvious challengers along with 2010 World Cup runners-up Holland.

BELOW Dirk Kuyt of Holland (left) celebrates with his team-mates after scoring the first goal, a penalty, against San Marino during a qualification match

REGIONAL CUPS

The speed with which football encircled the
globe as well as the rapid-fire popularity of the
World Cup inspired players, officials, and fans
from Chile to China. Each region soon created its
own governing body, which ultimately launched its
own "copycat" competitions for national teams.
The Copa America was the first, launched in
1916, and this was eventually copied in Africa,
Asia, Europe, and Oceania, plus Central
and North America.

REGIONAL CUPS
COPA AMERICA

The Copa America boasts the unique distinction of being the world's longest-running international football tournament. It began in July 1916 as part of Argentina's centenary independence celebrations.

ABOVE Argentina's midfielder Juan Roman Riquelme takes on Coloia in 2007

PAGE 76 The Uruguay team which won the 1917 Copa America

PAGE 77 Samuel Eto'o scores against Angola in the 2006 African Nations Cup

The competition was originally called the Campeonato Sudamericano de Selecciones (South American Championship of National Teams). Participation was limited initially to member nations of CONMEBOL, the South American football confederation. However, because the organization comprises only ten nations, the competition was expanded in 1993 to include invited participants from the Caribbean and North and Central America.

Usually two or three teams receive such an invitation, invariably one of them being Mexico, partly because of the geographical proximity and partly because of the lucrative television rights.

The United States have also been invited regularly since 1997, but have turned down the offer several times because of scheduling conflicts with Major League Soccer. However, they did accept an invitation for the 2007 tournament, ending a 12-year absence.

Until recently, the tournament used to take place every two years, but in 2007, CONMEBOL decided that it should be held every four years but in an odd-numbered year so that it did not clash with the World Cup and European Championship. The 2007 event took place in Venezuela, so a second rotation will begin in 2011, starting with Argentina. Uruguay and Argentina have each won the championship 14 times, followed by Brazil with eight. These totals exclude unofficial, early 20th-century competitions.

SOUTH AMERICAN CHAMPIONSHIP

In its early years, when it was known as the South American Championship, the tournament did much to popularize the game and raise standards of play across the continent.

The 1940s are regarded as its heyday, but a generation later it fell into neglect, because South America's military governments looked disparagingly at their neighbors. The national federations of major countries such as Brazil, Argentina, and Uruguay also began to question the wisdom of competing after scouts from Italy and Spain began to converge on the event and, almost before the final whistle had been blown, lured their star players away to Europe.

Most painfully hit were Argentina. They won the 1957 tournament on the inspiration of an outstanding inside-forward trio of Humberto Maschio, Antonio Valentin Angelillo, and Omar Enrique Sivori. The manner of their triumph prompted predictions of World Cup glory the following year. However, within months, all three had been spirited away to Italy; all three were even playing for Italy within three years.

The gradual return of democracy in the mid-1980s—coupled with the growing power of television—sparked a resurgence of interest in the competition, with the event played in a single country, rather than on a home-and-away basis.

Problems remain for South American administrators to resolve. The most important is the fact that the Copa is staged in the middle of the South American winter—which is also the close-season in Europe, where all the most glamorous players operate. Not only are European clubs reluctant to release their players, but the stars themselves are wary of the risk of burn-out. Thus Barcelona's Ronaldinho and Milan's Kaka both withdrew from the Brazilian squad heading for the 2007 event in Venezuela. As it happened, even without them, Brazil won the trophy. In the final they defeated Argentina for the second time in a row.

EXPLOSIVE FINAL

In 2004, in Lima, Brazil won on penalties after Argentina had twice taken the lead, the second time through substitute Cesar Delgado, with three minutes of normal time remaining. Adriano equalized in the third minute of stoppage-time with his seventh goal of the competition.

That goal sparked a brawl as Brazil's players celebrated in front of the Argentina bench. Argentina responded by squirting water at their opponents and referee Carlos Amarilla summoned riot-police to stop the trouble. Adriano was booked for removing his shirt.

Argentina seemed more unsettled by the incident and missed their first two penalties: Andres D'Alessandro fired his effort at goalkeeper Julio Cesar and Gabriel Heinze fired wildly over the bar. Brazil converted all their penalties, just as they had in their semi-final win over Uruguay.

In 2007, Brazil found it much easier. Argentina were favorites but never justified their status and subsided to one early spectacular goal from Julio Baptista, an unfortunate own goal by their own captain Roberto Ayala, and then a superb counterattacking strike from Dani Alves.

LEFT Brazilian players celebrate their victory against Argentina in 2007

REGIONAL CUPS
AFRICAN NATIONS CUP

Africa has become a magnet for cash-rich European clubs who are seeking an apparently unending source of talents. The biennial tournament has been played since 1957.

Players such as Didier Drogba, Samuel Eto'o, Michael Essien, and Jay-Jay Okocha have become superstars in Europe, using their experience and talents to inspire youngsters back home to follow in their footsteps. But it was not always the case. In the colonial era of much of the last century, European national teams brought African players such as Just Fontaine and Eusébio onboard for their own use.

Fontaine, born and brought up in Morocco, set a World Cup record of 13 goals in 1958 while representing France. Eusébio, born and brought up in Mozambique, finished as top scorer with nine goals for Portugal in the 1966 World Cup finals. But a move for change was already underway. Ten years earlier, in 1956, the Confederation of African

RIGHT Jay-Jay Okocha on the attack for Nigeria in the 2004 finals

BELOW South Africa's "Bafana Bafana" line up before their 2002 clash with Burkina Faso

Football had been organized in Lisbon and plotted a first Cup of Nations the following year in Khartoum, the capital of Sudan. It has since been staged virtually every two years, which makes it international football's African regional championship.

EGYPT IN SEVENTH HEAVEN

Only three nations competed in that first tournament. There should have been four but South Africa were barred because its government, wedded to the apartheid system, refused to approve the selection of a multiracial team. Ironically, 39 years later—after the downfall of apartheid—South Africa returned to rescue the confederation by staging the event after Kenya's late withdrawal as hosts.

Egypt, Ethiopia, and Sudan became the pioneer nations of a tournament that grew steadily down the years to encompass four, six, eight, 12, and eventually 16 finalists. In the early years, north African countries were the sides to beat, a trend that has been repeated half a century later, judging by the last three competitions.

Holders Egypt, the first African champions, have a poor World Cup record. However, they have won the African title a record seven times, most recently in Angola in 2010. Egypt, who beat Cameroon 1-0 in the 2008 final, pipped Ghana by the same score to deliver a record-breaking third consecutive final victory for coach Hassan Shehata.

Their hero was "supersub" striker Mohamed Nagy, better known as Gedo, who netted their 84th-minute winner against Ghana. He finished tournament top scorer with five goals, despite coming on as a substitute in all his side's six matches. He was on the pitch for a total of just 173 minutes.

However, the start of the tournament was overshadowed by tragedy when the driver and two members of the Togo party were killed in an attack on the team bus by separatist rebels. The Togo government then ordered the team to withdraw from the competition.

THE EARLY YEARS

Gedo follows in a tournament tradition of showcasing gifted individuals including heroes of yesteryear, such as the Ghanaian dribbling wizard Osei Kofi, Ethiopian captain Luciano Vassallo, and Egypt's skipper Rafaat Ateya. In that inaugural tournament he scored the very first goal in a 2-1 win over Sudan then scored all four in Egypt's 4-0 thrashing of Ethiopia in the final.

Organization of the second tournament was granted to Egypt and was contested by the same three nations. A last-minute goal saw Egypt retain the trophy with a breathtaking 2-1 win over Sudan.

Four teams met in Addis Ababa for the third edition, in 1962, with hosts Ethiopia seeing off the challenge of Egypt 4-2 in an exciting final. Ethiopia's last Emperor, Haile Selassie, handed over the cup to skipper Vassallo.

Eight nations took part in Ghana the following year, with a new format of an elimination round, semi-finals, and final. This format remained until 1976, when a second round league system was introduced.

Morocco won the 1976 edition, although the new formula proved unpopular and, in 1978, knockout semi-finals and a final were restored, along with penalty shoot-outs. Further alterations were made for the 1992 event in Senegal, when a dozen nations competed. By now the qualifying rounds were organized into mini-leagues rather than a straightforward knockout system.

A more recent expansion raised the number of entrants in the finals to 16, which proved popular with Africa's own nations but unpopular in Western Europe, where clubs resented being forced to relinquish their key players in the middle of their own league campaigns.

The most notable trend over the last two generations has been a significant shift of power, with West African nations challenging the domination of the northern countries.

FOOTBALL FACTS

RECENT WINNERS

1992 Host: Senegal, Winner: Ivory Coast
1994 Host: Tunisia, Winner: Nigeria
1996 Host and Winner: South Africa
1998 Host: Burkina Faso, Winner: Egypt
2000 Co-hosts: Nigeria/Ghana, Winner: Cameroon
2002 Host: Mali, Winner: Cameroon
2004 Host and Winner: Tunisia
2006 Host and Winner: Egypt
2008 Host: Ghana, Winner: Egypt
2010 Host: Angola, Winner: Egypt

ALL-TIME CHAMPIONS

Egypt (7); Cameroon, Ghana (4 each); Nigeria, Zaire/Congo DR (2 each); Algeria, Congo, Ethiopia, Ivory Coast, Morocco, South Africa, Sudan, Tunisia (1 each).

BELOW Didier Drogba enjoys Ivory Coast's progress to the 2006 semi-finals

Emad Moteb (3rd left) scoring the first goal for Egypt in their 2006 African Nations Cup Group A match against Ivory Coast

REGIONAL CUPS
OTHER NATIONAL TEAM COMPETITIONS

The history of national team competitions and their status as the ultimate peak of football achievement goes all the way back to the first official Scotland v England match on November 30, 1872. That goalless draw at Hamilton Crescent in Partick led to the creation of the British Home Championship.

RIGHT Ante Milicic strikes for Australia against the Solomon Islands in 2004

BELOW Harry Kewell leads the "Socceroos" to an easy win

Association football's first national team competition was staged annually until 1984, when it was killed off by dwindling crowds and the fixture congestion engendered by qualifying matches for the World Cup and European Championship.

At one stage, the British Home Championship also served as the World Cup qualifying section. That was after World War II, when the British associations—England, Scotland, Wales, and Northern Ireland—had rejoined FIFA after a gap of more than 25 years. FIFA designated two seasons of the British championship as the qualifying group. England finished top and went to Brazil in 1950. The runners-up were also granted a place in the finals, but the Scottish association said it would only send a team if they finished top of the group. They finished runners-up to England and duly stayed at home.

The British championship was put to the same use before the 1954 World Cup in Switzerland, but for the last time. Other nations objected that this gave the British a guaranteed place at the finals and the smaller British nations—Wales and Northern Ireland—complained that they were always going to be at a qualifying disadvantage against their larger neighbors. Ironically, for the next World Cup, "open" qualifying saw all four home nations go on to the finals, for the first and last time.

The awkward nature of international travel in football's early years was a significant factor

in the creation of regional competitions. Small, impoverished federations in days long before the advent of television and sponsorship could barely afford—or manage—to send a squad of players and handful of officials to a neighboring country for a tournament. Criss-crossing the world's oceans in an era when passenger flights were merely the stuff of science fiction would have been virtually impossible. Thus the South Americans set up their own tournament in the early 1900s, but it was not until the late 1950s that Europe and Africa dared go fully international.

THE GROWTH OF COMPETITIONS

A European national team competition had been organized in the 1920s and 1930s. This was the brainchild of Austrian and Hungarian football administrators, among them the Austrian Hugo Meisl, who also dreamed up the Mitropa Cup for the clubs of central Europe. The Gerö Cup was organized under the auspices of the world federation, FIFA, since a formal European federation was not brought into existence until the mid-1950s.

Elsewhere around the world, the desire for national team competition saw the fledgling central American confederation launch its own event in 1941; the first winners were Costa Rica. Further championships were staged only irregularly, even after the formal creation in 1961 of CONCACAF,

which finally bonded into one organization the various nations, large but mainly small, who made up the football world of central America (including some northern South American countries), the Caribbean and, of course, North America (which meant the United States and Canada).

The regional competition was eventually reorganized and stabilized, in 1991, as the Gold Cup. It takes place every two years. Mexico moved one ahead of the United States with five victories after beating an experimental USA team 5-0 in the 2009 final at Rutherford, New Jersey. Canada have won once, while none of the central American nations have won it at all.

Oceania remains the world game's poor relation in all senses, including competitive status. The region is FIFA's smallest, with only 11 members, and its standing within the world game was further reduced by Australia's departure in 2006 to join the Asian confederation. An Oceania Nations Cup was begun in 1973 but its diminished entry has placed its long-term future in doubt.

ASIAN CUP

RECENT WINNERS

1972 Iran
1976 Iran
1980 Kuwait
1984 Saudi Arabia
1988 Saudi Arabia
1992 Japan
1996 Saudi Arabia
2000 Japan
2004 Japan
2007 Iraq

ALL-TIME WINNERS:
Iran, Japan, Saudi Arabia (3 each); South Korea (2); Iraq, Israel, Kuwait (1 each)

CONCACAF GOLD CUP
(North, Central American, and Caribbean Nations)

RECENT WINNERS

1991 United States
1993 Mexico
1996 Mexico
1998 Mexico
2000 Canada
2002 United States
2003 Mexico
2005 United States
2007 United States
2009 Mexico

ALL-TIME WINNERS
Mexico (5), United States (4), Canada 1

OCEANIA NATIONS CUP
RECENT WINNERS

1973 New Zealand
1980 Australia
1996 Australia
1998 New Zealand
2000 Australia
2002 New Zealand
2004 Australia
2008 New Zealand

ALL-TIME WINNERS
Australia, New Zealand (4 each)

⚽ CLUB WORLD CHAMPIONSHIPS

WORLD CLUB CUP

RECENT WINNERS

2000 Boca Juniors (Arg) 2
Real Madrid 1 [World Club Cup]
Corinthians (Brz) 0
Vasco da Gama (Brz) 0
(Corinthians 4-3 on on pens)
[Club World Championship]
2001 Bayern Munich 1 (Ger)
Boca Juniors (Arg) 0
2002 Real Madrid (Spa) 2
Olimpia Asuncion (Par) 0
2003 Boca Juniors (Arg) 1
AC Milan (Ita) 1 (Boca Juniors 3-1 on pens)
2004 Porto (Por) 0
Once Caldas (Col) 0 (Porto 8-7 on pens)
2005 São Paulo (Brz) 1
Liverpool (Eng) 0
2006 Internacional (Brz) 1
Barcelona (Esp) 0
2007 AC Milan (Ita) 4
Boca Juniors (Arg) 2
2008 Manchester United (Eng) 1
Liga de Quito (Ecu) 0
2009 Barcelona (Spa) 2
Estudiantes (Arg) 1 (after extra time)

AC Milan have been crowned champions four times in the event's various guises. The competitions are now reformed after early years were marred by scandal and violence.

The Intercontinental Cup kicked off in 1960 as a home and away meeting between the champions of Europe and South America. The idea had sprung from South American officials, who had launched their own Copa Libertadores for the purpose of challenging Europe at club level.

Real Madrid were crowned the first winners. Their legendary team, inspired by Alfredo Di Stefano and Ferenc Puskás, drew 0-0 with Peñarol of Uruguay in torrential rain in Montevideo, then stormed to a 5-1 victory back in Spain. Within a matter of a few years, the competition almost ground to a halt, following a string of brutal matches involving Argentine sides. Celtic were furious at their treatment by Racing Club in 1967. A year later, Manchester United's maverick George Best lost his temper after incessant provocation by his marker José Hugo Medina of Estudiantes de La Plata and both were sent off.

Estudiantes, under coach Osvaldo Zubeldía, were notorious for their cynical tactics. In 1969, the Estudiantes players bombarded their Milan opponents with practice balls as they tried to warm up before the game in Argentina. Milan won 4-2 on aggregate, but three Estudiantes players received lengthy bans for their bad behavior.

RIGHT Milan's Pippo Inzaghi (Number 9) scores for Milan against Boca Juniors in 2007

Several European champions, such as Bayern Munich, Liverpool, and Nottingham Forest, declined to compete and the 1975 and 1978 contests were not held.

EIGHTIES REVIVAL

The competition was rescued in 1980, when the Japanese Football Federation, keen to promote the sport in the Far East, found sponsorship from car manufacturer Toyota to host the final as a one-off game. The inaugural showpiece was played in Tokyo until 2001, with neighboring Yokohama hosting the 2002 and 2004 finals.

The competition always mattered more to the South Americans than the Europeans. Even the wealthiest South American clubs could not match their European rivals in financial terms, so the Intercontinental Cup gave them a chance to underline a belief in their superior talent.

The last final in Tokyo's National Stadium saw Bayern Munich edge past Boca Juniors 1-0 in extra time. The final moved to Yokohama's new National Stadium the following year.

CLUB WORLD CHAMPIONSHIP

Meanwhile, FIFA had become directly involved in football at international club level. FIFA staged a Club World Championship in 2000 in Brazil. Noisily impatient clubs from outside Europe and South America were invited. European champions Manchester United even withdrew from the FA Cup to play, at the urging of the FA, which was bidding to host the 2006 World Cup. Corinthians beat Vasco da Gama 4-3 on penalties after the goalless all-Brazilian affair.

Due to various issues, the championship was not contested for the next four years. In 2004, FIFA decided to replace the Intercontinental Cup with an expanded mini-tournament and in 2005, it followed up its 2000 experiment. Japan remained, initially at least, as host nation. But no longer was the competition the preserve of the Europeans and South Americans. Brazil's São Paulo won the first of the revised events, beating European

champions Liverpool 1-0 in the final. They now had rivals which included Al-Ahly (Egypt), Al-Ittihad (Saudi Arabia), Deportivo Saprissa (Costa Rica) and Sydney (Australia).

The competition was renamed as the FIFA Club World Cup for the 2006 event and Internacional of Porto Alegre maintained Brazilian domination in 2006, beating Barcelona 1-0. Coach Abel Braga said: "Our club's history will now come under two headings, before and after Japan 2006!" Al-Ahly were there again in 2006, along with some new challengers: Auckland (New Zealand), Club America (Mexico), and Jeonbuk Hyundai (South Korea).

Milan's 4-2 victory over Boca Juniors in 2007 was Europe's first triumph since Porto's in 2004. Perhaps more significantly for the future, Japan's Urawa Reds took third place and African champions Etoile du Sahel were fourth.

Milan's victory signalled a change in the balance of power to Europe. Wayne Rooney scored Manchester United's winner against Liga de Quito in 2008, in the last tournament played in Japan. Abu Dhabi hosted the 2009 competition, won by Barcelona thanks to a thrilling comeback against Estudiantes. Gerard Pique leveled in the 89th minute and Lionel Messi chested home Dani Alves' cross for their extra time winner.

ABOVE Skipper Paolo Maldini and his Milan team-mates celebrate world domination

WORLD CLUB CUP

ALL-TIME CHAMPIONS
Milan (Ita) (4);

Boca Juniors (Arg), Nacional (Uru), Peñarol (Uru), Real Madrid (Spa), São Paulo (Brz) (3 each);

Ajax (Hol), Bayern Munich (Ger), Independiente (Arg), Internazionale (Ita), Juventus (Ita), Manchester United (Eng), Porto (Por), Santos (Brz) (2 each);

Atletico Madrid (Spa), Barcelona (Spa), Borussia Dortmund (Ger), Corinthians (Brz), Estudiantes (Arg), Feyenoord (Hol), Gremio (Brz), Internacional (Brz), Manchester Utd (Eng), Olimpia (Par), Racing (Arg), Red Star Belgrade (Ser), River Plate (Arg), Velez Sarsfield (Arg) (1 each)

Lionel Messi (right) scores the winning goal in Barcelona's 2-1 victory over Estudiantes de La Plata in the 2009 Club World Cup final

1960s

1970s

REGIONAL CUPS MOMENTS

ABOVE Liverpool's Steve Heighway on target against Servette

ABOVE The UEFA Cup is second in status to the Champions League

RIGHT Archie Gemmell scores Celtic's second goal during the 1970 European Cup final

ABOVE Colin Bell scores for Manchester City against Lierse

ABOVE Tottenham knock Milan out of the UEFA Cup in 1972

1970s

2000s

ABOVE Fans cheer Liverpool on to final victory over Borussia Mönchengladbach

ABOVE Corinthians celebrate their Club World Cup triumph in 2000

LEFT Liverpool in triumph after their golden goal win over Alaves in 2001

ABOVE A consolation goal for Wolves against Porto in 1974

RIGHT Alan Thompson's goal for Celtic knocks out Barcelona

INTERNATIONAL CLUB COMPETITIONS

The **UEFA Champions League** is the most lucrative international club competition ever to be played. It has evolved over the last 80 years, and there are further exciting changes planned for the future that will make matches more entertaining for fans. The original tournament was the **Mitropa Cup**—also known as the **La Coupe de l'Europe Centrale**. This was held among the leading clubs of central Europe during the late 1920s and 1930s. The European Champions' Club Cup was launched in the mid-1950s, along with the now renamed **UEFA Cup** and the defunct **UEFA Cup Winners' Cup**. Each contest has provided a flood of memorable goals, unforgettable moments, and great drama.

COUPE
CHAMPIONS
EUROPÉENS
Finale
1956

FOUNDATION & 1950s

"The Champions League is where every player wants to be."

KAKA OF MILAN

UEFA has come a long way since it was founded in Basel on 15 June 1954. It currently stands as the richest and most important of the six continental confederations of world governing body FIFA. UEFA oversees the numerous competitions from its headquarters in Nyon, a town on the shores of Lake Geneva in Switzerland.

EUROPEAN CUP

1950s FINALS
1956 Real Madrid 4 Reims 3
1957 Real Madrid 2 Fiorentina 0
1958 Real Madrid 3 Milan 2 (after extra time)
1959 Real Madrid 2 Reims 0

All the world's greatest players—from South America to southern Africa to south-east Asia—have a strong desire to play for European clubs, tempted by both the lucrative contracts and the chance of winning high-profile titles and medals.

UEFA was formed as a result of talks between the respective Football Federations of Belgium France and Italy. It was set up during the 1954 World Cup.

France's Henri Delaunay was the driving force. and immediately tackled the role of general secretary; Denmark's Ebbe Schwartz was voted in as the inaugural president.

UEFA grew hand in hand with the European Champions' Club Cup. This tournament was dreamed up by the then editor of the French sports daily newspaper *L'Equipe*, Gabriel Hanot, who became irritated by the claims of a

ABOVE The FIFA president, Sir Stanley Rous

RIGHT Red Star goalkeeper Beara foils a Manchester United attack

PAGE 92 Arie Haan is carried off the pitch by Ajax fans in 1971

PAGE 93 The victorious 1956 Real Madrid team celebrates

national English newspaper that Wolverhampton Wanderers—after beating Hungary's Kispest Honvéd in a friendly—were the champions of the world. Hungary had recently humiliated England 6-3 and 7-1.

So Hanot proposed a formal annual competition, but the concept proved so popular with the top clubs that the organisational work exceeded the newspaper's organising capacity.

In April 1955, UEFA agreed to take over the running of the European Champions' Club Cup. That decision laid the foundation for its power base, just in time. Later that month, three leading officials—Ernst Thommen (Switzerland), Dr Ottorino Barassi (Italy) and Sir Stanley Rous (England)—conceived the idea of the International Inter-Cities' Industrial Fairs Cup, the forerunner to today's UEFA Cup.

Three years later, UEFA introduced the European Nations' Cup and in 1960 the UEFA Cup Winners' Cup became a reality, running parallel with the European Champions' Clubs Cup.

The Champions' Club Cup, based on a two-leg knock-out system, grew from strength to strength despite severe problems with hooliganism, political turmoil, and stadium disasters. Lennart Johansson, the UEFA president between 1990 and 2007, was the man responsible for converting the Champions' Club Cup into the Champions League.

UEFA became a political player too, clashing with the European Union over television rights. Then came the Bosman Judgement, which established the primacy of EU labor law over football's own regulations and sparked the mass migration of leading players to Western Europe. In January 2008 Johansson was replaced as president by Michel Platini, the former France star who had won the Champions' Cup.

Real Madrid dominated the early European Champions' Club Cup, crowned winners at the first five successive wins. Santiago Bernabéu was the president who oversaw their phenomenal rise. He had the vision to raise Madrid's 20,000 capacity Chamartín ground and create a giant stadium that would house a great team. Bernabeu and his secretary Raimundo Saporta built that team. Their best signing was the Argentinian forward Alfredo Di Stefano. Madrid beat Barcelona to sign him from Colombian club Millonarios, aided by some help from the Spanish sports ministry.

Di Stefano was the pivotal figure in Madrid's success. He was the team's leader and finished league top scorer every season between 1955 and 1959. Madrid scaled the heights with a 7-3 victory over Eintracht Frankfurt in the 1960 final at Hampden Park, Glasgow. Di Stefano netted three, Puskas four.

BELOW Joseito, one of Real Madrid's home-grown Spanish heroes

EUROPE 1960s

Real Madrid launched a new European competitive decade in glory. Their 7-3 thrashing of Eintracht Frankfurt—West Germany's first finalists—in Glasgow in 1960 was hailed by experts as the greatest match of all time.

FOOTBALL FACTS

THE FINALS

1960 Real Madrid 7 Eintracht Frankfurt 3
1961 Benfica 3 Barcelona 2
1962 Benfica 5 Real Madrid 3
1963 Milan 2 Benfica 1
1964 Internazionale 3 Real Madrid 1
1965 Internazionale 1 Benfica 0
1966 Real Madrid 2 Partizan Belgrade 1
1967 Celtic 2 Internazionale 1
1968 Manchester Utd 4 Benfica 1,
after extra time
1969 Milan 4 Ajax Amsterdam 1

The inspirational Alfredo Di Stefano hit a hat-trick but was out-scored by Hungarian Ferenc Puskas who scored four goals. Madrid's five-year reign ended the next season, when they were beaten by Spanish rivals Barcelona. The Catalans had long envied Madrid their headline status in Europe; their success had been limited to a couple of victories in the lesser Inter-Cities' Fairs Cup.

They signed some of the world's finest players and coaches and believed their hour had come when, with the help of refereeing errors, they defeated Madrid in the opening rounds of the 1960–61 Champions' Cup.

Barcelona were then clear favorites to win the final but they were surprisingly beaten by Benfica from Lisbon. Two of Barcelona's stars, the Hungarian forwards Sandor Kocsis and Zoltan Czibor, had finished on the favorites' losing side at the same stadium in Bern, Switzerland, seven years earlier in the World Cup final against West Germany. Then, as now, the score was 3-2.

Benfica, unlike cosmopolitan Barcelona, relied solely on Portuguese players but this gave them the option of plucking many outstanding players from Portugal's African colonies. The most important was Eusebio da Silva Ferreira, from Mozambique, who scored two goals the following year when Benfica thrashed the aging maestros of Real Madrid 5-3 in Amsterdam. The Hungarian veteran Puskas ended up on the losing side despite scoring another Champions' final hat-trick.

A hat-trick of titles proved beyond Benfica, however, as the balance of power in Europe swung towards Italy and the city of Milan.

AC Milan overthrew Benfica in 1963, in the first European final at Wembley. Eusebio struck early for Benfica but was then played out of the game by Milan winghalf Giovanni Trapattoni as the Italians hit back twice through their Brazilian center-forward Jose Altafini. He thus finished with 14 goals in the campaign, then a record. Milan's creative inspiration came from their "Golden Boy" inside forward Gianni Rivera, supported by other Italian internationals such as captain and sweeper Cesare Maldini and winger Bruno Mora.

Milan's reign lasted only one season, however. They fell in the quarter-finals the next term to Real Madrid, who were, in turn, beaten 3-1 in the final in Vienna by Internazionale, Milan's city neighbors.

Inter were managed by master coach Helenio Herrera. In the spring of 1960 Herrera had been sacked by Barcelona after a European defeat at Madrid's hands. Now he enjoyed taking his belated revenge. Herrera was born in Morocco but brought up in Argentina. He became a professional footballer in France and had worked hard on the tactics, science, and psychology of football. At Inter he imposed a ruthless tactical system based on a rugged sweeper in Armando Picchi, man-marking defenders such

as Tarcisio Burgnich and Giacinto Facchetti, a perceptive playmaker in Luis Suarez and lightning counterattackers such as Sandro Mazzola and Jair da Costa.

Inter secured two cups—against Real Madrid in 1964 and Benfica in 1965—before Celtic and Manchester United struck the first blows for British football. In 1967 Scotland's Celtic, under the shrewd management of Jock Stein, carried all before them at home and abroad. Their brand of thrilling football swept aside even iron-clad Inter in the final in Lisbon. Not surprisingly, Celtic's team earned the nickname of the "Lisbon Lions."

One year later Manchester United marked the tenth anniversary of the Munich air disaster by seizing the trophy for the first time themselves. Matt Busby had built a remarkable new team, built around the inspiration of another Munich survivor Bobby Charlton. Charlton was partnered

ABOVE George Best celebrates United's second goal against Benfica

RIGHT Celtic's Billy McNeill takes delivery of the European Cup

in attack by George Best and Denis Law. Injury meant Law missed the final in which United beat Benfica 4-1 in extra time at Wembley, thanks to two goals from Charlton, now United's captain.

Their reign, however, lasted only one year. United were dethroned in the 1969 semi-finals by Milan— still led by Rivera—who then beat Holland's emerging Ajax Amsterdam in the final in Madrid's Estadio Bernabeu. Ajax were the first Dutch club to have reached the Champions' final. Their coach Rinus Michels was building a team and a style which would earn worldwide admiration. But their day had yet to dawn.

INTERNATIONAL CLUB COMPETITIONS
EUROPE 1970s

The 1970s was a European Cup decade which could be split into three reigns—those of Ajax Amsterdam, Bayern Munich, then the English. First though, in 1970, came Feyenoord of Rotterdam, Ajax's long-time rivals.

ABOVE Ajax Amsterdam, hat-trick winners in the early 1970s

Feyenoord, managed by the former Austrian international defender Ernst Happel, became the first Dutch team to win the trophy, beating 1967 winners Celtic 2-1. Sweden striker Ove Kindvall scored the winner four minutes from the end of extra time.

Ajax followed, with a vengeance. Their center forward Johan Cruyff was one of the all-time greats. His touch and vision inspired Ajax to three European titles and Holland to reach the 1974 World Cup Final.

Johan Neeskens was a tough-tackling, driving midfielder, Gerrit Muhren added craft, while Ruud Krol was a marauding leftback. In addition, coach Rinus Michels's players could switch positions in bewildering style in the formation known as "total

football." They won three finals, all comfortably. They defeated Panathinaikos of Greece 2-0 at Wembley put together their best performance of the three to defeat Internazionale 2-0 in Rotterdam, and then finished off with a 1-0 win over Juventus in Belgrade. Cruyff scored both goals against Internazionale.

It had been clear, however, that he would be lured away at some stage to Spanish football and that ultimately occurred in the summer of 1973 when Ajax reluctantly sold him to Barcelona for a then world record £922,000.

The departure of Cruyff left Ajax vulnerable to a challenge from German champions Bayern Munich, led by Franz Beckenbauer, a great creative midfielder who had perfected the role of attacking sweeper. Sepp Maier was a brilliant goalkeeper and Gerd Muller the greatest striker of his age. Muller scored 365 times in 427 Bundesliga appearances and 68 times in 62 games for West Germany.

Georg Schwarzenbeck was a defensive rock beside Beckenbauer, Paul Breitner was a gifted attacking full back, and Uli Hoeness was a clever forward. But Bayern had to battle for their three successive final wins. First opponents were Atletico Madrid in Brussels in 1974. Only a last-minute goal by Schwarzenbeck at the end of extra time earned a replay—the only one in the history of the competition—which Bayern won easily by 4-0. Leeds had a seemingly good goal disallowed before Franz Roth and Muller netted in the 1975 final; then Dominque Rocheteau hit the woodwork for Saint-Etienne ahead of Roth's winner a year later at Hampden Park, Glasgow.

Bayern grew old together—and the English succeeded them. The quiet, thoughtful Bob Paisley at Liverpool and the charismatic, and outspoken, Brian Clough at Nottingham Forest both built winning teams.

Liverpool's revival had been masterminded by Scottish manager Bill Shankly and Paisley, his assistant, was comparatively unknown when he took over in the summer of 1975. Very soon, however, it became clear that Paisley was a managerial giant. It was under his guidance that Liverpool won their first European Champions' Cup by defeating Borussia Monchengladbach 3-1 in the 1977 final in Rome.

At the time, Borussia were one of Europe's outstanding football teams under the guidance of meticulous coach Hennes Weisweiler and with an attack inspired by Denmark's first European Footballer of the Year, Allan Simonsen.

In Rome, however, Weisweiler's planning and Simonsen's energy proved no match for a Liverpool side, who had found a style pitched midway between the demands of frenetic English league football and the more thoughtful version demanded by European competition.

The match was a personal triumph for Liverpool's England right-winger Kevin Keegan, who memorably outwitted the Germans' terrier-like defender Berti Vogts.

It was Keegan's last game for Liverpool. Within weeks he had been sold to Hamburg and Liverpool used the fee to replace him with an even more outstanding player in Scotland forward Kenny Dalglish, bought from Celtic.

Dalglish emulated Keegan's success when, a year later, he scored the lone winning goal for Liverpool in their second Champions' final victory over Brugge of Belgium. Liverpool's reign ended early the next season with the success of the English team Nottingham Forest. Under the idiosyncratic management of the controversial Brian Clough, Forest went all the way to defeat Sweden's Malmo in the 1979 final. The decisive goal was scored by the England forward Trevor Francis.

Months earlier Francis had become Britain's first $2 million (£1 million) footballer when Clough bought him from Birmingham City. The Malmo game was his Champions' Cup debut.

LEFT John Robertson flies the flag for Nottingham Forest

FOOTBALL FACTS

THE FINALS
1970 Feyenoord 2 Celtic 1
(after extra time)
1971 Ajax Amsterdam 2
Panathinaikos 0
1972 Ajax 2 Internazionale 0
1973 Ajax 1 Juventus 0
1974 Bayern Munich 4 Atletico Madrid 0
(replay after 1-1 extra time draw)
1975 Bayern Munich 2 Leeds United 0
1976 Bayern Munich 1 Saint-Etienne 0
1977 Liverpool 3 Borussia
Monchengladbach 1
1978 Liverpool 1 Club Brugge 0
1979 Nottingham Forest 1 Malmo 0

EUROPE 1980s

"Heysel is a wound that cannot be healed."

MICHEL PLATINI

One event overshadowed the European Cup in the 1980s: the Heysel disaster of 1985. Thirty-nine fans, Italian and Belgian, were crushed to death as Liverpool fans attacked Juventus fans before a European Cup final in Brussels.

ABOVE The wrecked terracing at Heysel in 1985

It was Juventus' first Champions' Cup victory but that went almost unnoticed amid the carnage. Michel Platini, now UEFA president, and their star forward, said: "I'm physically and emotionally incapable of going back to Heysel. It's a wound that cannot be healed."

UEFA blamed Liverpool and their supporters. English fans had long been associated with hooliganism. UEFA banned all English teams indefinitely. That was later reduced to a five-year ban with an extra year for Liverpool.

UEFA and other officials were also punished by the Belgian legal system for a series of blunders, which extended from choosing an inadequate venue in the first place, to failure to ensure sufficient security controls. For instance, the wire fence which separated Liverpool and Juventus fans at the Heysel stadium was little more than chicken wire and easily breached.

In due course the Heysel—which had hosted previous Champions' Cup finals in 1958, 1966, and 1974—was razed. The King Baudouin Stadium was built in its place, in the shadow of the Atomium (this had been constructed for the world exhibition of 1958, which had been hosted by Brussels).

The tragedy was all the more shocking for English football since it took place only 18 days after 56 people had died in a fire at the Bradford City stadium. Not until after the 1989 Hillsborough disaster, however, were draconian measures finally put in place to improve security and safety at sports stadia. These were adopted across English sport and were just in time to avert the threatened introduction of a restrictive and potentially ruinous membership-card system.

English clubs had extended their domination of the European Champions' Cup throughout the early 1980s, in a series of low-key finals. First

Nottingham Forest extended their successful run to two years by defeating Kevin Keegan's Hamburg on a lone goal from Scotland winger Jimmy Robertson in 1980. Then Liverpool were equally cautious in beating Real Madrid the following year on a late goal from fullback Alan Kennedy. In 1982, Aston Villa pipped Bayern Munich also by 1-0, despite losing their keeper, Jimmy Rimmer, to injury early in the match. Center-forward Peter Withe scored the goal from close range, almost falling over the ball as he did so.

The only interruption to English command came from Hamburg who, inspired now by midfielder Felix Magath, beat Juventus 1-0 in 1983. It was a second win with a different club for Hamburg's Austrian coach, Ernst Happel. He had previously guided Feyenoord to victory in 1970.

Hamburg's reign did not last long however. In 2004, Liverpool returned to lift the trophy again; this time with a penalty shoot-out win over Roma on the Italians' home ground. The game marked the end of the love affair between Roma's fans and their Brazilian midfielder Paulo Roberto Falcao after his apparent reluctance to take one of the spot kicks.

The expulsion of English clubs from European competition in the second half of the 1980s left a gap which no one other European club could fill. Romania's Steaua Bucharest became the first eastern European winners on penalties against favorites Barcelona—coached by Englishman Terry Venables—in 1986. Porto beat Bayern 2-1 the following year; a result Uli Hoeness described as among the worst in Bayern's history. Holland's PSV Eindhoven shaded Benfica on penalties again in 1988.

Soon afterwards, real champions soon emerged in Italy's revived club Milan. The club had been refinanced in the mid-1980s by media magnate and future prime minister Silvo Berlusconi. He paid off the club's debts, invested heavily in Dutch stars such as Ruud Gullit, Frank Rijkaard, and Marco Van Basten.

ABOVE Marco Van Basten raises the reward for his two goals against Steaua

All three men had been instrumental in their country's 1988 European Championship victory.

Milan won the Italian league in 1988, then thrashed Steaua Bucharest in the following season's Champions' Cup final. The final was staged in Barcelona amid a TV blackout after local technicians went on strike. Berlusconi flew in staff from his own Italian TV channels to ensure that no-one in Europe should miss his team's achievement.

Already, however, the talismanic Van Basten was starting to become more vulnerable to a series of ever-more damaging injuries which would ultimately force him into premature retirement—he played his last game in 1993.

1950s　　1960s　1970s

ABOVE A derby goal for Alfredo Di Stefano (left) of Real Madrid against Atletico

BELOW Ferenc Puskas scores Real Madrid's first goal in the 1962 Champions' final against Benfica

ABOVE Ray Kennedy strikes for Arsenal in the 1979 Fairs Cup final

RIGHT George Best takes on the Benfica defence single-handed in 1968

ABOVE Chelsea's David Webb heads past Brugge keeper Luc Sanders

1980s

1990s

2000s

RIGHT Celtic's Lubomir Moravcik outwits the Juventus defense

BELOW Sol Campbell heads Arsenal in front against Barcelona in the 2006 Champions League final

BOTTOM Pippo Inzaghi grabs Milan's second against Liverpool in 2007

ABOVE Liverpool manager Joe Fagan relaxes with the European Cup

ABOVE Arsenal easily see off FK Austria in 1991

RIGHT Paolo Maldini in triumph after Milan's thrashing of Barcelona in 1994

INTERNATIONAL CLUB COMPETITIONS
EUROPE 1990s

The late 1990s marked the biggest change in the format of the European Cup since the competition was established more than 40 years earlier. No longer would it be a knockout competition for league champions.

From 1956 onward, the structure had been simple. The holders and the champions of each European county had met in a series of two-leg ties, leading to a one-match final. The team who scored most goals in the matches, home and away, progressed. It was a copy of the formula devised for the Mitropa Cup, which had proved hugely popular in central Europe in the 1930s.

BELOW Ole Gunnar Solskjaer wins the 1999 final for Manchester United

Initially, if scores were level after two matches a replay on neutral territory was organized. When it became more difficult to find neutral zones the clubs tossed to decide who would stage the replay. Eventually, however, the pressures of time led to the play-offs being scrapped—with the second leg of a balanced tie being extended into 30 minutes of extra time and then, if necessary, to a penalty shoot-out.

In 1991–92 this format was radically altered under pressure from wealthy clubs, including Real Madrid, Barcelona, Milan, Internazionale, Manchester United, Liverpool, and Bayern Munich. Extra clubs were admitted from the major nations and experiments began with a mini-league formula, until the present system—eight groups, then three knockout rounds before the final—was perfected.

These changes, which also raised the clubs' income through TV and sponsorship, were matched by another crucial development—the Bosman Judgement which, in December 1995, ruled that restrictions on the number of foreign players in any team and playing squad were illegal. The world's best players inevitably gravitated to a handful of rich European clubs, largely in England, Italy and Spain.

These changes were presided over by a Swedish president of UEFA, Lennart Johansson, who managed efficiently the difficult jobs of maintaining UEFA's control over the European competitions,

while simultaneously keeping the big clubs happy, largely thanks to the share of the revenue generated by the European competitions.

The drama of the European finals continued. One of the most dramatic moments came in 1999, when Teddy Sheringham and Ole Gunnar Solskjaer scored in the last seconds of stoppage time to lead Manchester United to an astonishing victory over Bayern Munich in Barcelona. Bayern had led by a single goal from Mario Basler for most of the match. United's victory secured them a historic treble of European Cup plus domestic league and FA Cup success, a unique achievement by an English club.

Johan Cruyff's "Dream Team" earned Barcelona's first Champions' Cup in 1992, when Ronald Koeman's rocket settled the contest against Sampdoria in extra time at Wembley. Fabio Capello's Milan then produced the finest performance of the 1990 finals when they unexpectedly came out in attack to rout Cruyff's Barcelona in 1994.

Surprisingly, Milan were beaten themselves a year later by a revived Ajax Amsterdam. Coincidentally, Ajax were guided to victory out on the pitch by the experienced string-pulling in midfield of Frank Rijkaard, a European Cup-winning hero with the Italian club in 1989 and 1990.

Ottmar Hitzfeld, a winning coach with Borussia Dortmund and Bayern, oversaw Dortmund's 3-1 success against Juventus in 1997 when Karlheinz Riedle scored twice, then fellow German Jupp. Heynckes guided Real Madrid to victory in 1998. Pedja Mijatovic scored Madrid's winner to secure their seventh Champions' Cup at the expense of favorites Juventus and their French midfield star, Zinedine Zidane.

Surprisingly, Heynckes was sacked by Madrid's impatient president Lorenzo Sanz on the grounds that the team had not, in addition, won the Spanish league. Sanz's unpredictable direction of

the club backfired when impatient fans voted him out of a job and voted in millionaire builder Florentino Perez.

The decade was not without its scandal. Olympique de Marseille became the first French champions of Europe in 1993. They beat Milan 1-0 in what would prove the last final in Munich's Olympic stadium. But their victory was tarnished by revelations that they had fixed matches to help secure their domestic dominance in France.

In particular, several Marseille players had been approached to fix a match the previous weekend, because a draw would secure the French league title for Marseille while also keeping their opponents, Valenciennes, within sight of safety at the other end of the table. Jacques Glassmann, one of the Valenciennes players who had been approached, informed his club's directors. A process was launched, which ended in a jail term for, among others, the Marseille president Bernard Tapie. Glassman, booed by French crowds in the aftermath, was awarded a FIFA Fair Play award in 1995 in recognition of his actions.

ABOVE Red Star Belgrade, first and last Yugoslav winners, in 1991

FOOTBALL FACTS

THE FINALS
1990 Milan 1 Benfica 0
1991 Red Star Belgrade 0 Marseille 0 (Red Star 5-3 on penalties after extra time)
1992 Barcelona 1 Sampdoria Genoa 0 (after extra time)
1993 Marseille 1 Milan 0
1994 Milan 4 Barcelona 0
1995 Ajax Amsterdam 1 Milan 0
1996 Juventus 1 Ajax 1 (Juventus 4-2 on penalties after extra time)
1997 Borussia Dortmund 3 Juventus 1
1998 Real Madrid 1 Juventus 0
1999 Manchester United 2 Bayern Munich 1

INTERNATIONAL CLUB COMPETITIONS
EUROPE 2000s

By 2000, the European Cup had become the Champions League, though not a league of champions. The format had been swayed heavily in favor of the elite clubs that made up the G-14 group from the major western leagues.

The wealthy western European leagues could enter three or four teams each season and dominated the competition. But it was not necessarily the teams which towered over their domestic leagues who lifted the European Cup/ Champions League. Only five winners since 1999—Bayern Munich in 2001, Barcelona in 2006 and 2009, Manchester United in 2008, and Internazionale in 2010—also won their domestic championships in the same season.

It was as if chasing a domestic championship and the Champions League was often a task too far. But a few clubs adapted ideally to the last 16 knock-out system. Liverpool, under Rafa Benitez, were the prime example. They won the Champions League in 2005, despite finishing 37 points behind Chelsea in the Premiership.

In 2007, when they lost to Milan, they ended up 21 points behind Manchester United. English critics claimed that Benitez knew Liverpool could not match the consistency of Chelsea or Manchester United; his season's strategy revolved around the latter stages of the Champions League.

Milan, meanwhile, also put all their eggs in the Champions League basket. The 2007 winners finished 36 points behind Serie A champions

RIGHT Delight for Milan's Kaka means despair for Liverpool

Internazionale. Both Liverpool and Milan rested and rotated players with the European Cup in mind, a pragmatic possibility often denied to their championship-chasing rivals.

Only once was the cycle of big clubs winning broken, when the favorites all went down in the 2004 quarter-finals. That left coach Jose Mourinho to guide Porto to an easy victory over Monaco.

The most dramatic final of the decade was staged in 2005 in Istanbul. Milan led Liverpool 3-0 at half time through Paolo Maldini's early goal and two strikes by Hernan Crespo. Steven Gerrard inspired Liverpool's fight back as he, Vladimir Smicer, and Xavi Alonso scored within seven minutes of each other to force extra time. The tie was settled on penalties. Andriy Shevchenko, Milan's winning penalty-taker in 2003 against Juventus, had his shot saved by Jerzy Dudek.

Spanish clubs also had their moments of glory.

Real Madrid had swarmed over Valencia in the all-Spanish final of 2000. Fernando Morientes, Steve McManaman, and Raul swept aside Hector Cuper's team. Caretaker boss Vicente Del Bosque had quelled the competing egos in the Madrid dressing room. He guided them to victory again in 2002, when Zinedine Zidane volleyed a magical winner against Bayer Leverkusen at Hampden Park, Glasgow.

Barcelona won in 2006 in Paris after teetering on the verge of defeat against Arsenal who went ahead through center-back Sol Campbell and held out until 13 minutes from time. Arsenal, ultimately, suffered for having to play much of the game with ten men after the early expulsion of their German goalkeeper, Jens Lehmann.

One factor in this decade had been a demonstration of the power of the big leagues. After an all-Spanish final in 2000 (Real Madrid beating Valencia) came an all-Italian final in 2003 (Milan beating Juventus) and then an all-English final in 2008.

The latter saw Manchester United win the crown for the third time after defeating Chelsea on penalties. United's success was perfectly timed

in the year which marked the 50th anniversary of the Munich air disaster. It was the first Champions League final to be staged in Moscow and the prospect of an invasion of English fans prompted the Russian authorities to make the unique concession of converting match tickets into visas.

The three failures in the shoot-out were committed by United's Cristiano Ronaldo and by Chelsea's John Terry and Nicolas Anelka. Ronaldo's miss was a surprise since he had scored a career-best 42 goals for United during the season.

He made his last United appearance in the 2009 final. But he could not help them retain the

prize, as goals from Samuel Eto'o and Lionel Messi clinched a 2-0 win for Barcelona and took the trophy back to Catalonia.

Mourinho—the "special one" as he styled himself—was a winner again in 2010. Diego Milito scored both goals as Internazionale beat Bayern Munich 2-0 in Madrid, to lift the trophy for the first time since 1965. Mourinho's side gave a master class in defensive organization, just as they had in the semi-final second leg in Barcelona. Mourinho had enjoyed the added satisfaction of knocking out his old club Chelsea in the last 16 too.

ABOVE Zinedine Zidane strikes his magnificent volleyed goal for Real Madrid in the 2002 final

Cristiano Ronaldo scores for Manchester United during the 2008 Champions League final against Chelsea

INTERNATIONAL CLUB COMPETITIONS
EUROPA LEAGUE, UEFA CUP & CUP WINNERS' CUP

The new Europa League, the UEFA Cup and the now-defunct Cup Winners' Cup have always been poor relations of the European Cup.

ABOVE Tottenham's John White, Bill Brown, Cliff Jones, Ron Henry, and Terry Dyson enjoy a happy homecoming to the UK in 1963

These were competitions for the "nearly" clubs who had fallen short of winning the major domestic trophy. Originally, the UEFA Cup was known as the Inter-Cities Fairs Cup. It was founded in 1955—a fortnight after the European Cup—by future FIFA president Sir Stanley Rous and vice-presidents Ottorino Barassi of Italy and Ernst Thommen of Switzerland.

With one eye on post-war rapprochement between Europe's former enemy nations, it was originally confined to representative teams whose cities staged trade fairs. Since the games were organized to coincide with the trade fairs, the first tournament lasted three years. The final was held in 1958, when a team made up entirely of

Barcelona players beat a London representative side 8-2 on aggregate over two legs.

Club teams were admitted to the next competition, and Barcelona beat Birmingham City 4-1 on aggregate in the 1960 final. Barcelona's heroes were the Hungarian Ladislav Kubala and Spain's own Luis Suarez. The competition was played annually after that. Initially, southern European clubs dominated, but Leeds' win in 1968 heralded a change. English teams (Newcastle, Arsenal, Leeds, Tottenham, and Liverpool) won the trophy for the next five years.

In 1971, the tournament was re-named after the European federation took formal control. The Fairs label was scrapped and the competition was called the UEFA Cup. Initially it continued as a two-leg knockout competition and the closing stages sometimes boasted a more glamorous mixture of clubs than the European Cup. Winners down succeeding years included Real Madrid, Internazionale, Juventus, and Roma.

Everything changed, however, with the development of the Champions League. The quality threshold dropped significantly with the departure from the UEFA Cup of the bigger second, third, and fourth-placed clubs (from their respective leagues) and the massive influx of clubs from the newly independent nations thrown up by the fragmentation of the Soviet Union and Yugoslavia.

UEFA also bowed to pressure from the clubs to produce a group stage which guaranteed three home matches for each club, while then allowing some teams that were knocked out of the Champions League entry into the UEFA Cup at the halfway stage for the knockout rounds. However, the system of five-team groups was unsatisfactory for fans and fixture patterns and was reorganized again in 2009.

Sevilla, under coach Juande Ramos, proved masters of the competition in 2006 and 2007, though they had to thank a spectacular shoot-out performance from goalkeeper Andres Palop for the second of their two victories, over fellow Spanish opposition in Espanyol.

An intriguing factor in the UEFA Cup has been evidence of the revival of Russian club football after the chaos that followed the collapse of the Soviet Union. CSKA Moscow won the UEFA Cup in 2005, beating Sporting Lisbon in front of their own fans, then Zenit St Petersburg beat Rangers in 2008.

Ukraine's Shakhtar Donetsk were the last UEFA Cup winners in 2009, before UEFA changed the name of the competition to the Europa League and extended the group stage to feature 48 clubs, each playing six matches. Diego Forlan scored both Atletico Madrid's goals as they beat Premiership side Fulham in the first final.

From 1999 onward, entrance into the UEFA Cup was also the formal reward for clubs who had won their national cups. This followed UEFA's decision to scrap the Cup Winners' Cup which had been running since 1960. The Cup Winners' Cup was always a poor relation because, while popular in Britain, the domestic knockout event had barely caught on in many other countries.

Italy's Fiorentina won the first final, beating Rangers of Scotland. Tottenham became the first British winners of a European competition when they defeated Atletico Madrid 5-1 in the final in 1963. The last final, in 1999, saw Italy's Lazio, coached by Sven-Goran Eriksson, beat Mallorca at Villa Park, Birmingham.

UEFA CUP

RECENT FINALS

2000 Galatasaray 0 Arsenal 0 (Galatasaray 4-1 on penalties after extra time)
2001 Liverpool 4 Alaves 4 (golden goal after extra time)
2002 Feyenoord 3 Borussia Dortmund 2
2003 Porto 3 Celtic 2 (silver goal after extra time)
2004 Valencia 2 Marseille 0
2005 CSKA Moscow 3 Sporting Lisbon 1
2006 Sevilla 4 Middlesbrough 0
2007 Sevilla 2 Espanyol 2 (Sevilla 3-1 on penalties after extra time)
2008 Zenit St Petersburg 2, Rangers 0
2009 Shakhtar Donetsk 2 Werder Bremen 1 (after extra time)

EUROPA LEAGUE

2010 Atletico Madrid 2 Fulham 1 (after extra time)

ALL-TIME WINNERS

(UEFA Cup and Fairs Cup)
Internazionale, Juventus, Liverpool, Valencia 3 each; Barcelona, Borussia Mg, Feyenoord, IFK Gothenburg, Leeds United, Parma, Real Madrid, Sevilla, Tottenham Hotspur 2 each; Ajax Amsterdam, Anderlecht, Arsenal, Bayer Leverkusen, Bayern Munich, CSKA Moscow, Dinamo Zagreb, Eintracht Frankfurt, Galatasaray, Ipswich Town, Napoli, Newcastle United, Porto, PSV Eindhoven, Roma, Schalke, Zaragoza, Zenit St Petersburg 1 each.

CUP WINNERS CUP

ALL-TIME WINNERS (1961–99)

Barcelona 4; Anderlecht, Chelsea, Kiev Dynamo, Milan 2 each; Aberdeen, Ajax Amsterdam, Arsenal, Atletico de Madrid, Bayern Munich, Borussia Dortmund, Everton, Fiorentina, Hamburg, Juventus, Lazio, Magdeburg, Manchester City, Manchester United, Mechelen, Paris S-G, Parma, Rangers, Sampdoria, Slovan Bratislava, Sporting Clube, Tbilisi Dynamo, Tottenham Hotspur, Valencia, Werder Bremen, West Ham United, Zaragoza 1 each.

ABOVE Andres Palop wins the 2007 UEFA Cup for Sevilla by saving Marc Torrejon's penalty

1963

2000s

ABOVE Eusébio thunders Benfica ahead against Milan in the 1963 Champions' final

ABOVE Real Madrid stars enjoy their 2000 Champions League triumph over Valencia

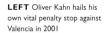

LEFT Oliver Kahn hails his own vital penalty stop against Valencia in 2001

ABOVE Jimmy Greaves takes Atletico Madrid apart to make history in 1963 Champions' final against Benfica

RIGHT Juan Riquelme (right) leads Boca Juniors to Libertadores glory against Cruz Azul

2000s

ABOVE Boca coach Carlos Bianchi leads the celebrations after victory over Santos

ABOVE Pepe Reina of Liverpool celebrates beating Chelsea in the 2007 semi-final

ABOVE Ever Alfaro of Deportivo Saprissa takes Mexico's Pachuca by surprise

BELOW Liverpool players hail their victory over Milan in 2005

RIGHT Ronaldo heads Manchester United ahead against Chelsea

BELOW David Beckham on MLS duty for Galaxy against Chivas

The Copa Libertadores dé América is the South American equivalent of the European Cup. The winners tackle their European counterparts for the honor of becoming the world's greatest club.

ABOVE Boca captain Diego Cagna strikes a cup-winning pose in 2003

The Copa Libertadores grew out of a tournament of seven South American champions, played in Santiago de Chile in 1948 and won by the Brazilian club Vasco da Gama.

A dozen years later the Copa Libertadores was launched as an annual tournament. South American club directors, notably those of Peñarol from Uruguay, had seen the success of the European Cup and wanted a version of their own. Once the Copa Libertadores was established, then the vision was to eventually introduce an annual series matching the champions from Europe and South America against each other for the world club crown.

The Copa Libertadores kicked off in 1960 with the participation of the champions from Argentina, Bolivia, Brazil, Chile, Colombia, Ecuador, Paraguay, Peru, and Uruguay. Peñarol were crowned champions after defeating Paraguay's Olimpia 2-1 on aggregate. Pedro Spencer, the free-scoring Ecuadorian striker, was Peñarol's inspiration and went on to become the most prolific marksman in the history of the competition.

Peñarol, happily fulfilling their original ambition, went on to arrange a world club showdown with their European counterparts Real Madrid. However, the Spanish side steamrollered them 5-1 in Madrid after a 0-0 draw in Montevideo.

Peñarol bounced back to be crowned South American champions the following season, but then they were toppled by Brazilian outfit Santos.

The legendary Pelé proved the inspiration for Santos, who also won two years in a row and saw off the first serious Argentine challenge from Boca Juniors.

Although Peñarol and Montevideo rivals Nacional would both win the Copa Libertadores again, Uruguay's pre-eminence faded and the tournament is currently dominated by clubs from Argentina and Brazil. Their supremacy has been interrupted only by a trio of wins for Olimpia, two successes apiece from Colombia's Atlético Nacional and Once Caldas and single triumphs by Chile's Colo Colo and Liga de Quito of Ecuador.

Over the years the Copa Libertadores has featured a string of dramas—from crowd pitch invasions to 20-plus penalty shoot-outs and some of the most cynical football imaginable. Culprits for the latter were the Argentinean club Estudiantes de La Plata in the late 1960s. Under influential coach Osvaldo Zubeldía, they took anti-football to a cynical new low.

Originally the competition involved only the national champions. But the Copa Libertadores was soon opened up to two teams from each country. The simultaneous introduction of a first-round group stage also assisted with travel costs, as the two clubs from whichever country would be drawn in the same group as the two clubs from another country. This meant teams could travel together and, for convenience, play their matches on successive days.

LEFT Hugo Ibarra (left) sends Robinho flying in Boca's 2003 victory over Santos

COPA LIBERTADORES

RECENT FINALS (OVER TWO LEGS)

2001 Boca Juniors (Arg) 1 Cruz Azul (Mex) 1 (on agg, Boca 3-1 on penalties)

2002 Olimpia (Par) 2 Sao Caetano (Brz) 2 (on agg, Olimpia 4-2 on penalties)

2003 Boca Juniors (Arg) 5 Santos (Brz) 1 (on agg)

2004 Once Caldas (Col) 1 Boca Juniors (Arg) 1 (on agg, Once Caldas 2-0 on penalties)

2005 Sao Paulo (Brz) 5 Atletico Paranense (Brz) 1 (on agg)

2006 Internacional (Brz) 4 Sao Paulo (Brz) 3 (on agg)

2007 Boca Juniors (Arg) 5 Gremio (Brz) 0 (on agg)

2008 LDU Quito (Ec) 5 Fluminense (Brz) 5

2009 Estudiantes de La Plata (Arg) 2 Cruzeiro (Brz) 1 (on agg)

2010 Internacional (Brz) 5 Guadalajara (Mex) 3 (on agg)

ALL-TIME WINNERS

Independiente (Arg) (7); Boca Juniors (Arg) (6); Peñarol (Uru) (5 each); Estudiantes de La Plata (Arg) (4); Nacional (Uru), Olimpia (Par), São Paulo (Brz) (3 each); Cruzeiro (Brz), Gremio (Brz), Internacional (Brz), River Plate (Arg), Santos (Brz) (2 each); Argentinos Juniors (Arg), Atletico Nacional (Col), Colo Colo (Chi), Flamengo (Brz), Liga de Quito (Ec), Once Caldas (Col), Palmeiras (Brz), Racing (Arg), Vasco da Gama (Brz), Velez Sarsfield (Arg) (1 each)

The tournament expanded in the 1970s, allowing Argentina and Brazil five clubs each along with three teams each from other countries—including new participants, Venezuela and Mexico. Mexico does not belong to the South American confederation and are guests in the competition. Their best ever showing was Cruz Azul's run to the 2001 final when they lost to Boca Juniors.

Boca, winners of the Copa Libertadores in 2000, 2001, 2003, and 2007, can lay claim to being the dominant club of South American soccer's new century. Brazilian clubs offer Boca's only real challenge, often led by three-time winners São Paulo. However, Liga de Quito pulled off a major surprise in the 2008 final, becoming the first Ecuadorian winners and earning a place in FIFA's Club World Cup in Japan.

Opponents, Brazil's Fluminense were also in the final for the first time and were red-hot favorites. Liga won the first leg, 4-2, at altitude in Quito.

Fluminense fought back to level on aggregate, winning the return 3-1 in Rio de Janerio's Maracanã Stadium, but paid a literal penalty for complacency. The contest was decided by penalty kicks, which Liga won 3-1, courtesy of three saves by veteran goalkeeper José Cevallos.

Estudiantes won for the fourth time in 2009. It was their first triumph since 1970 and they became the first side to triumph after starting in the preliminary round. They drew their home leg of the final, against Brazil's Cruzeiro, 0-0, then staged a winning comeback after falling behind in Belo Horizonte. Gaston Fernandez leveled, and Mauro Boselli netted his eighth goal of the competition for Estudiantes' winner. That made him tournament top scorer.

In the 2010 competition Internacional of Brazil won both legs of the final to defeat Mexico's Guadalajara 5-3 on aggregate and claim their third title.

INTERNATIONAL CLUB COMPETITIONS
REST OF THE WORLD

The contest between national champions is not confined to Europe and South America. Central and North America started its own championship in 1962. Africa followed two years later. Asia began its continent-wide challenge in 1967. Only the Oceania confederation held back, until 2004–05. But the defection of Australia to the Asian confederation in 2006 robbed the tournament of its strongest team.

AFRICAN CHAMPIONS LEAGUE

RECENT WINNERS
2003 Enyimba (Nigeria)
2004 Enyimba (Nigeria)
2005 Al-Ahly (Egypt)
2006 Al-Ahly (Egypt)
2007 Etoile Sahel (Tunisia)
2008 Al-Ahly (Egypt)
2009 TP Mazembe (Congo Dem Rep)
2010 TP Mazembe (Congo Dem Rep)

LEADING ALL-TIME WINNERS
Al-Ahly (Egypt) (6); Zamalek (Egypt)
(5); Canon (Cameroon), Hafia Conakry
(Guinea), Raja Casablanca (Morocco)
(3) each

ASIAN CLUB CUP

RECENT WINNERS
2003 Al-Ain (United Arab Emirates)
2004 Al-Ittihad (S Arabia)
2005 Al-Ittihad (S Arabia)
2006 Jeonbuk Motors (S Korea)
2007 Urawa Red Diamonds (Japan)
2008 Gamba Osaka (Japan)
2009 Pohang Steelers (S Korea)
2010 Seongnam Ilhwa Chunma (S Korea)

LEADING ALL-TIME WINNERS
Pohang Steelers (S. Korea) (3); Esteghlal
(Iran), Al-Hilal (S Arabia), Al-Ittihad (S
Arabia), Maccabi Tel-Aviv (Israel), Thai
Farmers Bank (Thailand) (2 each)

The central American competition has long been dominated by Mexican clubs. Teams from North America have yet to make an impact, despite the emergence of Major League Soccer and David Beckham's move to LA Galaxy. The biggest challenge to Mexican supremacy has come from Costa Rica. LD Alajuelense and Deportivo Saprissa have both proved recent powers in the tournament.

Interest in the CONCACAF club competitions was enhanced by the creation first of the Copa Interamericana and then by the expansion of the Club World Championship. The Copa Interamericana pitched the winners of the CONCACAF Champions League against the champions of South America, the winners of the Copa Libertadores.

Early in the 21st century FIFA scrapped the old Club World Cup, contested by the champions of Europe and South America, and replaced it with the Club World Championship into which the winners of all the regional club competitions were guaranteed entry.

Clubs from the Arab north have historically dominated the African Club Championship. Egypt's Al-Ahly from Cairo have been the team to beat. Their toughest opponents have been the Tunisian side Etoile du Sahel. Other major rivals have come from West Africa, a prominent recent recruiting ground for Western European clubs. Perhaps this is one reason for the North African clubs' success: they do not lose as many players to Europe as their neighbours.

Southern Africa has yet to make its mark, despite boasting some of the richest and most passionately supported clubs on the continent, such as Kaizer Chiefs and Orlando Pirates, South Africa's only winners in 1995. A major disappointment for South African fans has been that its clubs have not made a greater impression at international level.

Israeli teams dominated the early years of the Asian competition. Maccabi Tel-Aviv won twice and Hapoel once, before the Israelis were forced out for political reasons. The Arab-dominated Asian confederation expelled Israel, whose clubs remained absent from international competition for almost 30 years. Israel joined UEFA in the 1990s after which its clubs entered the European competitions.

In the meantime, middle-eastern sides had taken command of the Asian club tournaments until the development of the rich new leagues in both Japan and South Korea. The J.League side Urawa Red

Diamonds underlined the power of the J.League when they became Asian champions in 2007 after beating Sepahan from Iran. They succeeded Jeonbuk Hyundai Motors, who ended the Arab supremacy in 2006.

J.League side Gamba Osaka defeated Australia's Adelaide United home and away in the 2008 final. South Korea's Pohang Steelers won a record third title by beating Al-Ittihad from Saudi Arabia 2-1 in the one-match 2009 final in Tokyo.

The Japanese and Koreans have gained in strength thanks to importing European and South American coaches, and also from the experience the best of their players have gained in Europe. The Middle East countries largely missed that international exchange, partly because their clubs could pay the players so well there was no financial incentive for them to seek a move to Europe.

Africa, Asia—now strengthened by Australia — and central/North American have already shown they can challenge the traditional powers. But Oceania seems destined to remain a backwater and may struggle to retain its place in the Club World Championship.

The FIFA president, Sepp Blatter, has said: "We want everyone to take their place in the greatest competitions but we also have to protect the status and value of those competitions."

LEFT Etoile de Sahel guard the African Super Cup

BELOW LEFT Pachuca players celebrate after beating Los Angeles Galaxy in a shoot-out in 2007

OCEANIA CLUB CHAMPIONSHIP

RECENT WINNERS

2005 Sydney FC (Australia)
2006 Auckland City (New Zealand)
2007 Waitakere United (New Zealand)
2008 Waitakere United (New Zealand)
2009 Auckland City (New Zealand)
2010 PRK Hekari United (Papua New Guinea)

CENTRAL/NORTH AMERICAN CLUB CUP

RECENT WINNERS

2003 Toluca (Mexico)
2004 LD Alajuelense (Costa Rica)
2005 Deportivo Saprissa (Costa Rica)
2006 America (Mexico)
2007 Pachuca (Mexico)
2008 Pachuca (Mexico)
2009 Atlante (Mexico)
2010 Pachuca (Mexico)

LEADING ALL-TIME WINNERS

America (Mexico), Cruz Azul (Mexico) (5 each); Pachuca (Mexico) (4); Deportivo Saprissa (Costa Rica), UNAM (Mexico) (3 each)

GREAT NATIONS

International power in football is defined by
a mixture of achievement and history. Success
or failure at the World Cup finals is what counts
to today's modern critic, followed by titles in the
various regional championships. Brazil boast five
World Cup victories, one more than mighty Italy.
Germany have scored a hat-trick of successes on
the world stage, with Argentina and Uruguay twice
crowned as world champions, while England and
France have each triumphed once. The role of the four
British Home Nations is acknowledged worldwide,
especially as England are major crowd pullers.

GREAT NATIONS
BRAZIL

England may have invented the modern game, but Brazil —and Edison Pelé in particular—have perfected it to such an extent that they can now boast a record-breaking five World Cup wins.

ABOVE Brazil team in 1970

PAGE 118 Brazil star Garrincha skips past Wales defender Terry Hennessey in 1962

PAGE 119 The 1986 France team before their match against Canada

Few dare argue with the Brazilian pre-eminence in modern football—especially after watching the timeless re-runs of Garrincha and Pelé swaggering their way to Brazil's first World Cup win in 1958 or, 12 years later, witnessing the color-soaked TV scenes from Brazil's third World Cup triumph in the Mexican sunshine.

Since then, successive generations of Brazilians have consistently lived up to Pelé's romantic notion of "the beautiful game." But the original link was an English one. In 1894, Brazilian Charles Miller, whose father was originally from England, brought over

the first footballs to be seen in Brazil, after a study trip in Southampton where he was taught the game. Its popularity swiftly spread and Brazil can now boast the proud achievement of being the only nation to have competed in every World Cup finals tournament.

The country's first footballing hero was Arthur Friedenreich, who, in the early part of the 20th century, was popularly supposed to have been the first senior player to score over 1,000 goals. Emulating him was Leonidas, who spearheaded Brazil's attack at the 1938 World Cup finals in France. Unwisely, the coach, Ademar Pimenta, decided to rest Leonidas from the semi-final against World Cup title holders Italy in order to be fresh for the final—which, of course, Brazil never reached.

Brazil were awarded hosting rights to the next World Cup finals, but its realization had to wait until after World War II. It was originally due to be played in 1949, but a mixture of European uncertainty and slow preparation work put the staging back to 1950. Brazil reached the final only to suffer a shock 2-1 defeat to Uruguay in front of almost 200,000 disbelieving fans. As Brazil had lost the final while dressed in all-white, they superstitiously decided to make the switch to their current strip of yellow shirts and blue shorts—arguably today's most famous football kit.

Brazil reached the quarter-final stage at the 1954 World Cup finals in Switzerland, returning to Europe to take the world title in Sweden four years later with almost an entirely new team. Coach Vicente Feola had brought in the mercurial outside right Garrincha and a 17-year-old inside left called Pelé.

As a teenage sensation, Pelé shared top billing for Brazil with wizard dribbler Garrincha, nicknamed "the Little Bird," and the midfield duo of Didi and Zito. In 1970, Pelé was complemented by the likes of Gerson, Roberto Rivelino, Tostao, and explosive Jairzinho—the only player to score in every match in every round at the World Cup finals. When Pelé retired in 1977, he boasted more than 1,000 goals in a career with Brazil, Santos, and New York Cosmos.

Brazil had to wait for 24 years to claim their fourth World Cup, edging past Italy on penalty kicks at the 1994 finals in the United States. Brazil's Bebeto and Romario were the deadliest strike pairing at the tournament going into the final, yet the match finished goalless.

Ronaldo was a member of the 1994 squad but did not play and, in 1998, he was hampered by injury and illness as Brazil surrendered their crown to France. Yet he was the two-goal hero in the 2002 final victory over Germany and in 2006 became the World Cup's all-time leading scorer.

Brazil's immense size long hindered the development of a national league until 1971, and the traditional old regional championships still generate fierce rivalry. Flamengo and Fluminense insist that they are the best-supported clubs, although São Paulo have a record six league titles.

The wealth of Brazilian football has always rested on the Rio-São Paulo axis, with the country now the world's greatest exporter of players. Most members of Brazil's recent World Cup squads have been European-based, a stark contrast to 1958 and 1962, when their entire squads played for Brazilian clubs.

Santos have been the most internationally acclaimed club in Brazilian football history. This is largely due to their perpetual global touring in the 1960s, when they cashed in on the fame and

ABOVE Pelé in action against Italy in the 1970 World Cup final

drawing power of Pelé. Despite the touring, Santos at their peak were a fine team that in 1962 and 1963 won both the Copa Libertadores and the Club World Cup.

Outstanding Brazilian coaches have included World Cup-winning managers Feola, Aimoré Moreira, Mario Zagallo, Carlos Alberto Parreira, and Luiz Felipe Scolari, as well as Claudio Coutinho, Sebastião Lazaroni, and Tele Santana.

Heroes have included Kaka, the 2007 World Player of the Year, and Cafu—the only player to have featured in the final of three consecutive World Cups (1994, 1998, and 2002). Rivaldo and Ronaldinho were the attacking stars of that 2002 side.

FOOTBALL FACTS

CHAMPIONS—LAST TEN YEARS
2000 Vasco da Gama
2001 Atlético Paranaense
2002 Santos
2003 Cruzeiro
2004 Santos
2005 Corinthians
2006 São Paulo
2007 São Paulo
2008 São Paulo
2009 Flamengo

GREAT NATIONS
ARGENTINA

Argentina took until 1978 to lift the World Cup despite producing legendary coaches, players, and teams. Their greatest player was the controversial Diego Maradona, who inspired them to a second world title in 1986. So it was remarkable that it took so long before the talented men in the distinctive blue-and-white stripes won their first World Cup.

Argentina had come close to the title before, but finished as runner-up in the inaugural 1930 finals to hosts Uruguay. In 1978, it took home advantage, plus brilliant goals from Mario Kempes, the midfield promptings of Ossie Ardiles, and shrewd managerial guidance by César Luis Menotti to fire them to victory.

They added a second crown at the 1986 World Cup finals in Mexico. This time they were inspired by Maradona, who had failed to make the successful 1978 squad due to a lack of experience.

Argentina then finished as runners-up to West Germany at the 1990 World Cup finals, despite Maradona's talents being restricted by his knee injury.

Maradona's slide from glory continued at the 1994 World Cup finals in the United States, when he failed a dope test and was immediately sent home in disgrace. In his absence, Argentina bowed out to Romania in the second round. They reached the quarter-final stage four years later, crashed out in the first round in 2002 and made it to the quarter-finals in 2006.

Despite a controversial career, Maradona remains an idol for his outrageous talent and the sheer nerve with which he scored a remarkable two goals against England in the 1986 World Cup finals. These goals are legendary. One was helped in with his hand. He scored the other after a solo run from the halfway line.

Argentina have played a major role in the history of the Copa Libertadores, the South American equivalent of Europe's Champions League. Seven Argentine clubs have won the trophy— Independiente (seven times), Boca Juniors (six),

BELOW Alfredo Di Stefano scores for Real Madrid

Estudiantes (four), River Plate (three), Racing Club, Argentinos Juniors, and Velez Sarsfield (one each). Boca Juniors and River Plate are among the world's greatest clubs, with the majority of the country's finest players having used them as a springboard to lucrative careers in Europe.

In the late 1940s, River carried all before them with a forward line nicknamed La Maquina—"The Machine"—for its prolific goal-scoring. They fielded two inside forward stars, Juan Manuel Moreno and Angel Labruna, while in reserve was a young Alfredo Di Stefano. The side broke up in the early 1950s, when Argentine players went on strike in a demand for improved contracts. Many, including Di Stefano, were lured away to a "pirate" league in Colombia and never returned.

Boca became the first Argentine club to reach a South American club final in 1962, but narrowly lost to Pelé's Santos in the Copa Libertadores. Independiente, from neighboring city Avellaneda, became Argentina's first Continental champions in 1964 and Racing Club were crowned as the country's first Intercontinental Cup champions in 1967.

Argentina have won the Copa America 11 times, most notably in 1957 when the inspirational performances of inside forward trio Humberto Maschio, Antonio Valentín Angelillo, and Omar Sivori established them as early favorites to win the following year's World Cup. By the 1958 World Cup finals, the trio had been sold to Italian clubs and Argentina's hopes went with them.

From then on, a steady stream of Argentine players headed for the riches on offer in Europe. By the mid-1990s, as most Western European countries eased their restrictions on foreign players, a minor industry grew up in "finding" European forebears—and European Union passports—for many Argentine players.

The recent Argentine influence at the top of the Champions League has been huge. Forward Lionel Messi, the undoubted star of Barcelona's 2009 winning team, was voted World Player of

the Year. The following season, four Argentines—skipper Javier Zanetti, center back Walter Samuel, midfielder Esteban Cambiasso, and striker Diego Milito—played key roles in Internazionale's victory. Milito emphasized the point by scoring both goals in Inter's 2-0 win over Bayern Munich in the final.

Meanwhile, the domestic game has been split down the years by a clash of styles. In the 1960s and 1970s, coaches such as Juan Carlos Lorenzo (Boca), Manuel Giudice (Independiente), and Osvaldo Zubeldía (Estudiantes), ruthlessly put the achievement of results above quality and entertainment. Yet the country's football federation deserved enormous credit for appointing the more positive Menotti as coach. Under Menotti, Argentina's triumph and style of play at the 1978 World Cup finals inspired a significant shift in opinion.

FOOTBALL FACTS

CHAMPIONS—LAST TEN YEARS
2001 Boca Juniors / San Lorenzo
2002 Racing Club / River Plate
2003 Independiente / River Plate
2004 Boca Juniors / River Plate
2005 Newell's Old Boys / Velez Sarsfield
2006 Boca Juniors / Boca Juniors
2007 Estudiantes / San Lorenzo
2008 Lanus / River Plate
2009 Boca Juniors / Velez Sarsfield
2010 Banfield / Argentinos Juniors

Note: two league seasons per year

BELOW Maradona's "hand of God" goal against England in 1986

> "We play to win, otherwise what's the point?"
>
> PAOLO ROSSI

Italy has tasted glory on the world stage with four World Cup crowns. A dramatic penalty shoot-out won them the final against France in 2006—12 years after they lost the World Cup to Brazil on penalties.

ABOVE Luigi Riva outpaces Brazil defender Brito in the 1970 World Cup final

Italy is second only to Brazil in terms of World Cup wins. Known as "the Azzurri," or "Blues," the national side also triumphed at the 1968 European Championship, but this has been their lone triumph at confederation level. They came close, however, in 2000. Under the management of former World Cup-winning goalkeeper Dino Zoff, they lost 2-1 to France on the "golden goal" rule in Rotterdam.

A combination of English and Swiss students and teachers introduced the sport to Italy in the second half of the 19th century, with the English influence still evident in the anglicized style of club names such as AC Milan and Genoa (rather than Milano and Genova).

Their national league was founded in the late 1920s, and top Italian clubs took part with limited success in the Mitropa Cup—an inter-war predecessor of the modern-day competition known as the Champions League.

Turin-based Juventus proved to be the outstanding side of the 1930s, winning the league title five years in a row and providing the backbone of the national team that won the World Cup in 1934.

Italy had refused to play in the 1930 World Cup finals in Uruguay, but won the next two world crowns thanks to the managerial wisdom of Vittorio Pozzo and the genius of inside forward Giuseppe Meazza. Pozzo played three Argentines in the team that beat Czechoslovakia in the 1934 final. Pozzo responded to criticism by pointing

out their eligibility for national service, saying: "If they can die for Italy, then they can play football for Italy!"

Torino also won five consecutive titles in the 1940s with an outstanding squad that was so strong the national team used ten of their players in one match. However, the Torino squad was destroyed by the Superga plane crash in May 1949, as they returned from a testimonial match in Lisbon.

The Torino disaster wrecked Italy's prospects ahead of their World Cup defence in Brazil in 1950 and had far-reaching effects. In 1958, Italy failed for the first time to progress through the qualifiers into the World Cup finals.

During the early 1960s, clubs such as AC Milan and their bitter rivals Internazionale ruled the European scene, even though the national team were unable to follow suit. Italy's participation in the 1966 World Cup finals remains notorious for their 1-0 defeat at the hands of North Korea, one of football's biggest upsets.

Adversity turned to glory when Italy captured the 1968 European Nations Cup after a replay. And two years later, inspired by the legendary figures of Giacinto Faccheti, Sandro Mazzola, Gigi Riva, and Gianni Rivera, Italy took part in one of the greatest games ever played. They edged past West Germany 4-3 in extra time to secure a place in the final of the World Cup. But they were so exhausted after the victory in the altitude of

ABOVE Dino Zoff defies Brazil's Roberto and Oscar

RIGHT Paolo Rossi hails Alessandro Altobelli's third goal in the 1982 World Cup Final

Mexico that they surrendered 4-1 to Brazil.

Italy arrived at the 1982 World Cup finals in the wake of a match-fixing scandal. Coach Enzo Bearzot and veteran captain Zoff imposed a press blackout. Paolo Rossi had just returned from a two-year ban for his alleged role in the scandal and proved to be their inspiration, with six goals—including a hat-trick against Brazil—guiding his nation to victory.

For the next 24 years, the leading league clubs kept the Italian flag flying at international level with a string of European trophies.

Pride was finally restored at national team level in 2006 when, after Zinedine Zidane's infamous head butt, Italy became world champions again by beating France in a penalty shoot-out in Berlin. Yet this triumph was partially overshadowed by another match-fixing scandal that saw a number of teams, including Juventus, relegated as punishment to Serie B. Juventus had been under investigation for the illegal administration of unspecified

stimulants to their players when telephone-tap investigators uncovered a match manipulation system created by the club's "transfer king" Luciano Moggi.

Evidence suggested that Moggi had used his influence with referees to generate yellow and red cards and suspensions for opposing players before they were due to face Juventus.

AC Milan beat Liverpool 2-1 to lift the European Cup in 2007 and restore some credibility for the Italian club game. Three years later, Internazionale won the trophy for the first time since 1965, sweeping aside Bayern Munich 2-0 in the final in Madrid. Yet coach Jose Mourinho's starting line-up did not include one Italian.

FOOTBALL FACTS

CHAMPIONS—LAST TEN YEARS

1999 AC Milan
2002 Juventus
2003 Juventus
2004 AC Milan
2005 (not awarded: Juventus title revoked)
2006 Internazionale
2007 Internazionale
2008 Internazionale
2009 Internazionale
2010 Internazionale

GREAT NATIONS
NETHERLANDS

**Dutch football is synonymous with "total football"—
the all-action strategy pioneered by Ajax Amsterdam
under the inspiration of center forward Johan Cruyff in
the early 1970s.**

While Cruyff provided the brains and leadership out on the pitch, Ajax's coach Rinus Michels masterminded the strategy. With two fabulous feet and mesmeric ball skills, Cruyff was at the heart of the Holland team—all of their goals in the 1974 World Cup finals either started or ended with a contribution by their captain.

Cruyff was supported by Johan Neeskens in midfield, Ruud Krol from full back, and the duo of Johnny Rep and Rob Rensenbrink in attack. At the peak of their success, the team were nicknamed "Clockwork Orange," after the color of their shirts as well as their precision passing. They again finished as runner-up at the World Cup finals, even without Cruyff, in 1978.

Yet in terms of international status, Holland had been late developers. A crucial reason was the fact that it was not until the mid-1950s that domestic clubs such as Feyenoord, Sparta, and Excelsior—notably all from Rotterdam—forced the recognition of professionalism, even initially part-time. The amateur status that ruled the Dutch game previously meant that star players, such as Faas Wilkes, had been forced abroad to the likes of Italy and Spain to earn a living from their talent.

Feyenoord became the first Dutch club to reach the semi-final stage of the European Cup in 1963, when they lost narrowly to Benfica. This was the start of a remarkable era, during which Feyenoord won the domestic double—league and cup—in both 1965 and 1969.

They became the first Dutch club to win a European crown in 1970, edging past Celtic in extra time with a team that included outside left Coen Moulijn—one of the finest of Dutch players before the Ajax era.

Later Feyenoord, while largely playing second fiddle to Ajax at home, won the UEFA Cup twice. In recent years, PSV Eindhoven have also been regular group stage contenders in the Champions League, reaching the semi-finals in 2005.

Holland's national team had not qualified for the World Cup finals since 1938, but the entire international status of Dutch football was about to change with the eruption of Ajax, which had reached the 1969 European Cup final and won it in 1971, 1972, and 1973, before Cruyff was sold to Barcelona.

Cruyff bowed out of international football at the end of 1977 but Holland continued to produce an endless stream of talented players and coaches.

PSV Eindhoven won the 1988 European Cup under the wily management of Guus Hiddink, while Holland—under Michels—won the European Championship in West Germany six weeks later. The Dutch national hero at that time was AC Milan—and former Ajax—striker Marco van Basten, who scored a group stage hat-trick against England, a semi-final winner against West Germany, and a magnificent volleyed winning goal against the Soviet Union in the final in Munich.

But too often at major tournaments, Holland's

potential has been undermined by squabbling between players and coaching staff over tactics and team selection. Inspirational forward Ruud Gullit, a former World and European Player of the Year, refused to play for Holland at the 1990 World Cup finals. Manager Hiddink sent midfielder Edgar Davids home during Holland's involvement in the 1996 European Championship after internal squabbling among the squad.

The unpredictability of the Dutch game's biggest names was evident up to the spring of 2008. Van Basten, by now manager of Holland, agreed to return as coach to Ajax after the European Championship in Austria and Switzerland, with Cruyff as a senior consultant. However, Cruyff had barely been confirmed in the role before he withdrew in an apparent disagreement with Van Basten—his one-time protégé—over youth strategy.

This is a sector that has become more crucial than ever to the Dutch game. The Ajax youth set-up is famed worldwide, with its players coached in a style and tactical system imposed on all the teams right through to the senior professionals. The club raises significant income selling players to the big leagues in England, Italy, and Spain to supplement its income from regular annual participation in European competitions.

Ajax remain serious contenders in domestic football, though PSV have declined after losing stars to wealthier leagues. But the championship successes of unfashionable Alkmaar in 2009 and Twente in 2010 illustrate the changing balance of power in the Dutch game.

ABOVE Johan Cruyff, captain and center forward of Holland and Ajax Amsterdam in the early 1970s

1960s

1970s

GREAT NATIONS **MOMENTS**

RIGHT Pelé celebrates Brazil's first in the 1970 World Cup final victory

BELOW Fabio Capello (front, left) lines up for Italy against England in 1973

ABOVE North Korea and Portugal emerge for their sensational 1966 World Cup tie

BELOW The Soviet Union greet their English host fans in 1966

RIGHT Franz Beckenbauer betters rival captain Johan Cruyff in the 1974 World Cup final

1970s 1980s 1990s 2000s

ABOVE Argentina poised to win their first World Cup, in 1978

RIGHT England line up, optimistically, ahead of their 1982 World Cup assault

BELOW Holland in 1978 —about to finish World Cup runners-up once more

ABOVE Didier Six opens up for France against Czechoslovakia in 1982

ABOVE Mexico head for a 2-1 defeat by Portugal in Germany in 2006

LEFT Gary Lineker's penalty goal against West Germany in 1990 is not enough for England

GREAT NATIONS
ENGLAND

England lays justifiable claim to be the home and birthplace of football—the game itself is thought to originate in the Middle Ages, but its rules weren't formalized until the mid-19th century.

The formation of the Football Association in 1863, the first FA Cup Final in 1872, and the introduction of a revolutionary league system in 1888 were major events in the game's development.

But England has only one World Cup triumph to date; the 1966 success at London's Wembley Stadium. This victory was founded upon Alf Ramsey's coaching, Bobby Moore's captaincy, Bobby Charlton's long-range shooting, and Geoff Hurst's famous hat-trick. Bobby Robson's team, inspired by Paul Gascoigne and Gary Lineker, came closest to tasting success again by reaching the 1990 World Cup semi-final in Italy.

Despite international disappointment, England has some of the world's richest and most watched domestic teams. The national game's image was marred by hooliganism and the Hillsborough tragedy in the 1980s. But booming television revenues and the lucrative FA Premier League's 1992 launch have helped tempt over some of the world's top talents. Manchester United have dominated the Premier League era, with big-spending Chelsea recently competing for a slice of glory.

United claimed England's first European Cup by beating Benfica in 1968, some five years after

RIGHT England Captain Bobby Moore plants a winning kiss on the World Cup in 1966

Bill Nicholson's Tottenham had become the first English winners of a European trophy in the Cup Winners' Cup. Under the management of Sir Alex Ferguson, United won a unique hat-trick for an English club in 1999, with victory in the Premier League, FA Cup, and the Champions League.

Another Champions League triumph followed in 2008, when United defeated Chelsea in a penalty shoot-out in Moscow in the first all-English final in the competition's history.

English clubs had previously dominated Europe in the late 1970s and early 1980s, winning the European Cup for six successive years.

The dark side of the English passion for football has been a long history of hooliganism. Trouble began to be noted in the early 1970s, and English fans' passion for traveling to away matches meant that hooliganism was exported. Leeds United were barred from European football in the mid-1970s after their fans, angered by controversial refereeing in the 1975 European Cup final against Bayern Munich, ripped out seats in the Parc des Princes in Paris.

A string of incidents occurred over the next decade. After the Heysel disaster of 1985—when 39 Juventus fans died in Brussels after being charged by Liverpool followers—both football and the law took action. The process was expanded after a crowd crush disaster at Hillsborough, Sheffield, in 1989. All-seater demands were imposed on all major sports venues, leading to the building of new grounds and total redevelopment of others. The pace of the stadia and security revolution persuaded UEFA to grant England hosting rights to the European Championship finals in 1996, which proved a huge success on and off the pitch.

English football has led the world game in many ways. In the late 1920s it was Arsenal, thanks to manager Herbert Chapman and forward Charlie Buchan, who conceived the "WM" system, a formation that dominated the sport for four decades. In the early 1990s, England opened the way for foreign investors and owners, also creating

ABOVE David Beckham lines up England's winning penalty against Argentina in 2002

the FA Premier League at a crucial time when satellite television was booming and clubs were turning to the London Stock Exchange.

Enormous controversy was generated by the purchase of Manchester United by the American Glazer family, although concerns about the club's debt were soon overshadowed by their continuing success on the pitch.

Chelsea emerged as United's major rivals after the remarkable takeover in 2003 by Russian oligarch Roman Abramovich, who invested seemingly limitless sums in paying off the club's debts and buying some of the world's finest players. Abramovich's early rewards included Premier League titles in 2005 and 2006.

Chelsea also won the English Premiership and cup double under ex-Milan boss Carlo Ancelotti in 2010, thus ending United's run of three successive titles and denying them the chance to achieve a historic fourth in a row. United are still tied with Liverpool on 18 championships apiece.

GREAT NATIONS
FRANCE

France's contribution to football goes far beyond its national team's significant achievements on the pitch. French administrator Jules Rimet was the brains behind the creation of the World Cup finals.

FOOTBALL FACTS

CHAMPIONS—LAST TEN YEARS

2001 Nantes
2002 Lyon
2003 Lyon
2004 Lyon
2005 Lyon
2006 Lyon
2007 Lyon
2008 Lyon
2009 Bordeaux
2010 Marseille

Another French administrator, Henri Delaunay, paved the way for the European Championships. Gabriel Hanot, editor of the daily sports newspaper L'Equipe, was the creative force behind the European Cup.

France's greatest achievement on the field was their World Cup victory, on home soil, in 1998. Inspired by midfielder Zinedine Zidane, they saw off Paraguay, Italy, and Croatia in the knock-out stage before crushing Brazil 3-0 in the final.

Two years later, David Trezeguet scored the "golden goal" that beat Italy 2-1 in the 2000 European Championship final. Sylvain Wiltord had forced extra time with a last-gasp equalizer.

Zidane, who retired from international football after the 2004 European Championships, made an impressive comeback as France reached the final of the 2006 World Cup, but was sent off for head butting an opponent during defeat by Italy.

One of the greatest personalities in the modern French game has been Michel Platini. In 1984, he towered over the Euro finals—in France—scoring nine goals as the home team went on to beat Spain 2-0 in the final. Later, Platini progressed to become the country's national manager, President of the Organizing Committee of the 1998 World Cup and then a Counsellor to FIFA President Sepp Blatter before being elected UEFA president in 2007.

French club football is often overshadowed by the national team, as so many home-grown players have moved abroad. One of the persistent problems for the league has been the lack of an established, successful club in the capital, Paris. The power of the French game has resided largely in the provinces. The comparatively new team Paris Saint-Germain once reached the final of the now-defunct European Cup Winners' Cup, but are

RIGHT Raymond Kopa, the first French footballer to be hailed European Player of the Year

better known for a long series of boardroom and ownership battles.

The first French club to make an international impression were Reims. Prompted by creative center forward Raymond Kopa, they reached the first European Cup final in 1956 and were losing finalists again three years later. Kopa was the playmaker for the France side that finished third in the 1958 World Cup finals and helped set up most of Just Fontaine's record tally of 13 goals. Fontaine had been brought in only at the last minute because of injury to Reims team-mate René Bliard.

No French club managed to reach the European Cup final again until the emergence of Olympique Marseille in the late 1980s and early 1990s. The team were bankrolled by the flamboyant businessman-turned-politician Bernard Tapie.

A team starring top-scoring French player Jean-Pierre Papin and England winger Chris Waddle finished as runner-up in the 1991 European Cup, losing on penalties to Red Star Belgrade. Two years later, Marseille defeated AC Milan 1-0 with Papin playing for the Italian club. But that triumph was tarnished almost immediately as Marseille were thrown out of European competition over a domestic match-fixing scandal that saw Tapie imprisoned.

Other French football clubs and their directors were punished, with sentences ranging from suspensions to fines for financial irregularities. Lyon president Jean-Michel Aulas said: 'What we need in the French game is greater financial freedom to run our own affairs. Then maybe we wouldn't have these other problems.'

Software millionaire Aulas knew his subject well. He had taken over Lyon when the club were in the second division, and supplied both financial and administrative resources to secure promotion and then a record run of seven successive league titles from 2002 to 2008.

Aulas even pressed successfully for a relaxation of laws barring sports clubs from obtaining outside, foreign investment. He claimed that, without new

revenue streams, French clubs could not afford to buy the best players nor could they develop stadia to such an extent that the country could ever hope to host the finals of the World Cup or European Championship.

The factor that has continued to elude Aulas has been European success. Lyon have regularly reached the Champions League knock-out stage but have never progressed to the final. They eliminated Real Madrid to enter the 2010 semi-finals, but lost 1-0 to Bayern Munich in Germany and sank 3-0 at home.

Saint-Etienne (1976) and Monaco (2004) remain the only other French clubs aside from Reims and Marseille to have reached a European Cup final. Saint-Etienne lost narrowly to Bayern Munich while Monaco crashed 3-0 to Porto.

BELOW Zinedine Zidane outplays Italy's Gennaro Gattuso in the 2006 World Cup final

GREAT NATIONS
GERMANY

"After the game is always before the next game."

SEPP HERBERGER

Germany have long been one of the most powerful countries in international football and their leading club, Bayern Munich, are one of the most famous, thanks to four European Champions' Cup victories.

FOOTBALL FACTS

CHAMPIONS—LAST TEN YEARS

2001 Bayern Munich
2002 Borussia Dortmund
2003 Bayern Munich
2004 Werder Bremen
2005 Bayern Munich
2006 Bayern Munich
2007 Stuttgart
2008 Bayern Munich
2009 Wolfsburg
2010 Bayern Munich

Bayern reached their eighth final in 2010, after winning the domestic league and cup double. But Internazionale beat them 2-0 in Madrid, thus scuppering their treble dream.

Football had difficulty establishing itself initially in Germany because of the social strength of the gymnastic movement. Attitudes changed gradually—partly because of football's popularity among young people—and clubs thrived in the inter-war years despite constant tension over the issue of professionalism. Even under Hitler's National Socialist government in the 1930s, football was considered a recreation with payments to players prohibited. This did not prevent many clubs from bending the rules.

The leading club in the 1930s were Schalke, which came from the mining town of Gelsenkirchen in the Ruhr. All their players were paid as miners. Their star winger Ernst Kuzorra revealed years later: "The nearest we saw of a mine was the pithead in the distance."

The German game was organized in a regional championship, topped off by a play-off series to decide the national champions. The play-off final regularly drew crowds of 70,000–80,000. Schalke were crowned champions six times and won the domestic cup once in the 1930s. Their inside forward, Fritz Szepan, led Germany to third place in the 1934 World Cup. Kuzorra and Szepan both have roads named in their honor around the present Schalke stadium.

After the war, political reality saw Germany divided into west and east sectors. Ultimately, Soviet-supported East Germany developed its own football federation and league. Although East Germany became a force in international swimming and athletics, it did not replicate this success in football. East Germany only ever qualified for the World Cup finals in 1974, and in the same year, Magdeburg won the nation's only European club trophy by taking the Cup Winners' Cup.

In contrast, football in West Germany went from strength to strength. Wily coach Sepp Herberger and captain Fritz Walter guided the West German team to a shock victory over hot favorites Hungary in the final of the 1954 World Cup. The victory was known as the "miracle of Berne." Hungary had not been beaten for four years. Further World Cup triumphs followed in 1974 and in 1990.

In 1990, the collapse of the Berlin Wall led to the reunification of Germany and the integration of East German football into the German football federation, which had always styled itself as the "overall" Deutscher Fussball Bund.

Germany, whether West or unified, have also finished as World Cup runner-up four times (1966, 1982, 1986, and 2002) and third three times (1976, 1992, and 2008). They have also won the European Championship three times (1972, 1980, and 1996) and three times finished as runner-up (1976, 1992, and 2008).

A significant factor in the national team's success was the creation of the unified, fully professional Bundesliga in 1963. Bayern Munich, who have won 22 modern championships to add to their all-Germany success in 1932, hold the record for the greatest number of domestic titles. The greatest personality to emerge from within Bayern was Franz Beckenbauer, known as "Der Kaiser."

As captain and sweeper, Beckenbauer led Bayern Munich to a European Cup hat-trick (1974, 1975, and 1976). He was ably supported by a host of stars that included goalkeeper Sepp Maier, full-back Paul Breitner, midfielder Uli Hoeness, and the greatest goalscorer of the modern era, Gerd Müller, who netted 68 goals in 62 games for his country, including the winner in the 1974 World Cup final against Holland.

Bayern won the trophy for a fourth time in 2001, when Ottmar Hitzfeld repeated his success as Borussia Dortmund coach in 1997. Hamburg, in 1983, were the other German victors.

Beckenbauer later coached West Germany to 1990 World Cup victory over Argentina in Italy, having guided them to the final four years earlier. Later, he coached Bayern Munich to UEFA Cup success in 1996 and became their president in time to oversee their 2001 triumph.

Moving on up the political ladder, Beckenbauer led the German bid to win hosting rights to the 2006 World Cup finals for Germany and was then president of the FIFA Organizing Committee. As a vice-president of the German Football Federation he was also voted onto the executive committees of both FIFA and UEFA.

TOP Hosts West Germany await kick-off in the 1974 World Cup finals

BOTTOM Bayern's Gerd Müller pounces on a defensive slip

GREAT NATIONS
PORTUGAL

The Portuguese team are often known as the "Brazilians of Europe," thanks to the flamboyance of Eusébio in the 1960s, the "golden generation" of Luis Figo, João Pinto, and Rui Costa in the 1990s, and the country's latest idol, Cristiano Ronaldo.

FOOTBALL FACTS

CHAMPIONS—LAST TEN YEARS

2001	Boavista
2002	Sporting Lisbon
2003	Porto
2004	Porto
2005	Benfica
2006	Porto
2007	Porto
2008	Porto
2009	Porto
2010	Benfica

Traditionally the Portuguese game has been dominated by the three leading clubs—Benfica, Porto, and Sporting Lisbon. Only Belenenses in 1948 and Boavista in 2001 have broken their monopoly of the league since its formation in 1934. Benfica lead the way with 32 championships, with Porto picking up 17 of their 24 titles in the past 26 years.

Football was introduced to Portugal through the ports in the 19th century, but the relatively small size of the country meant the national team had little or no impact internationally. However, Portugal had a source of playing talent in its African territories, such as Angola and Mozambique. An increasing number of African players were imported by the clubs and, from the late 1950s, also selected for the national team. Such players included Benfica's goalkeeper Jose Alberto Costa Pereira, striker Jose Aguas, and the two inside forwards Joaquin Santana and Mario Coluna.

All four were members of Benfica's European Cup-winning side that, in 1961, defeated favorites Barcelona 3-2 in Berne. Simultaneously, Benfica had also acquired the greatest African discovery of all in young striker Eusébio da Silva Ferreira. One year later he scored two thundering goals as Benfica defeated Real Madrid 5-3 to win their second European Cup. Eusébio would also lead Benfica to three more finals, albeit finishing on the losing side against AC Milan (1963), Internazionale (1965), and Manchester United (1968).

A mixture of Sporting Lisbon's defense, along with Benfica's midfield and attack, provided the backbone for the Portuguese national side that finished third in their first ever World Cup finals in 1966 with Eusébio the tournament's nine-goal top scorer.

Like the country itself, Portuguese football suffered from economic decline in the following decades but a new era dawned with triumphs in the 1989 and 1991 World Youth Cups. Ever since the emergence of the so-called "golden generation," Portugal became a potential threat at major tournaments.

FAR RIGHT Eusébio floors Hungary's defence in the 1966 World Cup finals

RIGHT Cristiano Ronaldo escapes Germany's Philipp Lahm at Euro 2008.

Porto emerged as the dominant club under the controversial presidency of Jorge Nuno Pinto da Costa. He hired an equally controversial coach in Jose Mourinho. He was rewarded with victory in the 2003 UEFA Cup and then, more impressively, in the Champions League a year later. Mourinho was lured away to Chelsea that summer.

Portugal reached the semi-final stage of the 2000 European Championship in Belgium and Holland. The inability to compete in wages with the giants of England, Italy, and Spain meant the departure of stars such as Figo (Barcelona, Real Madrid, and Internazionale), Simao Sabrosa (Barcelona and Atletico Madrid), Deco (Barcelona and Chelsea), and Cristiano Ronaldo (Manchester United and Real Madrid). But the national team gained technically and tactically from these players competing in better-quality leagues.

From 2003–08, the Portuguese Football Federation hired Luiz Felipe Scolari, Brazil's 2002 World Cup-winning coach, to bring the best out of the country's depth of talent. He was only a qualified success. Portugal finished as runner-up on home territory in the 2004 European Championship—losing to outsiders Greece in the final—and were fourth at the 2006 World Cup finals in Germany. Scolari's final game was at the 2008 European Championship, when Portugal fell 3-2 to Germany in the quarter-finals. Critics claimed the team had been distracted by the mid-event announcement of Scolari's new job at Chelsea and by uncertainty over Ronaldo's proposed move from Manchester United to Madrid.

Scolari conceded on leaving in 2008 to return to club football: "I did not win something big which is what I came to do."

GREAT NATIONS
SPAIN

World and European champions Spain are enjoying the finest period in their international history, after decades of underachievement. Andres Iniesta's extra-time winner in the 2010 World Cup final against Holland clinched Spain's greatest triumph. Two years earlier, Fernando Torres hit the decider against Germany in the Euro 2008 final.

RIGHT Captain Fernando Olivella and coach Jose Villalonga, European winners in 1964

Spain have a history rich in great players. Now their current stars—goalkeeper and captain Iker Casillas, midfielders Cesc Fabregas, Xavi Hernandez, and Iniesta, and the strike force of Torres and David Villa—can claim equality in the hall of fame with older heroes. These include legends of the1920s and 1930s, when goalkeeper Ricardo Zamora, defender Jacinto Quincoces, and inside forward Luis Regueiro helped Spain become the first foreign nation to beat England—4-3 in Madrid in 1929.

At the end of the 1950s, a team packed with stars such as Alfredo Di Stefano, Ladislav Kubala, and Luis Suarez saw Spain ranked as favorites to win the inaugural European Nations Cup. However, when the 1960 quarter-final draw matched Spain against the Soviet Union, dictator Francisco Franco ordered the team to withdraw on political grounds. Even so long after the Spanish Civil War, Spain still had no diplomatic relations with countries from the Communist Bloc.

In 1964, on home soil, Spain won its first international title. Relations with the East had thawed significantly enough for the USSR squad to be allowed entry into Spain for the European Championship finals. Strikers Jesus Pereda and Marcelino each scored in Spain's 2-1 victory over the Soviets.

Spain's failure to achieve international success in the next 44 years remains one of football's mysteries. The football federation had long run one of the most successful international youth sections. But the best the seniors could point to was a runner-up spot at the 1984 European Championship finals and a 5-1 win over Denmark in the second round of the 1986 World Cup finals,

ABOVE Fernando Torres heads for glory against Germany in 2008

when Emilio Butragueno, nicknamed "the vulture," scored four goals.

However, at club level the story could not be more different. Real Madrid were Europe's first club champions in 1956 and retained the trophy for the next four years, during a period of total domination. With nine European Champions Cups, two UEFA Cups, and 31 domestic league titles, Real Madrid have their own special place in the history books.

They also led the way in European stadium development, which they owed to the vision of Santiago Bernabeu, who became president in 1943. Bernabeu issued bonds to finance the building of a new super stadium that was opened in 1947. Its capacity was increased in the late 1950s to 125,000, as fans flocked to watch their heroes.

However, Barcelona—the Catalan institution—stands not far behind. With its motto of "More than a Club," Barcelona claims a unique loyalty on and off the field. Yet Barca has never dominated the European Cup in the manner of their bitter rivals.

But they have won it three times, beating Sampdoria 1-0 in extra time at Wembley in 1992, then seeing off Arsenal 2-1 at the Stade de France in 2006. Their great team of 2009 completed a treble—domestic league and cup plus the European Cup—by beating Manchester United 2-0 in the final in Rome. But they could not become the first team to retain their crown in the Champions League era. They lost 3-2 on aggregate to Internazionale in the 2010 semi-finals, after a stormy second leg in the Nou Camp.

Spain's goalkeeper Iker Casillas (center) makes a spectacular save during the 2010 World Cup final

GREAT NATIONS
RUSSIA

Europe's most populous nation has rarely punched its weight in international football. So far, its greatest days came in the early 1960s, while it was a part of the Soviet Union.

Moscow, capital of the old USSR, was once the central force in its national football. It boasted all the major clubs—Dynamo, Spartak, Torpedo, Lokomotiv, and CSKA—and the finest players. The size of the country made it difficult for any other clubs to compete effectively until air travel was possible. Even that was a risk, with the entire first team squad of Pakhator Tashkent killed when their plane crashed in 1979.

By the mid-1960s, however, major powers were emerging in the club game in Georgia and Ukraine especially, and also in Armenia and Belarus.

Dynamo Tbilisi, Dynamo Kyiv, Dynamo Minsk, and Ararat Yerevan may have owed their creation to the Soviet model but all developed a style very different to the physical Moscow approach. Tbilisi and Kyiv played with a Latin touch of flair. Kyiv twice won in the European Cup Winners' Cup and Tbilisi won it once—but they never co-existed happily with the Moscow factions.

The Soviet Communist attitude to sport brought other complications. The USSR ignored FIFA and would not compete internationally until after World War II. A tour of Britain by Moscow Dynamo in the winter of 1945 marked a slight thaw. Two years later the Soviet Union joined FIFA on condition that it could have a permanent vice-president.

Soviet footballers were supposedly amateurs, not paid for playing though they were paid for their nominal roles in the armed services or other professions. The Soviet Union felt free to send its strongest possible team—the so-called "state amateurs"—to the Olympics, while western rivals were weakened by the transparency of their own players' professional status. The Soviet national team competed internationally for the first time at the 1952 Olympic Games, which they duly won four years later in Melbourne. Their heroes were world-class footballers, goalkeeper Lev Yashin and left-half skipper Igor Netto.

Yashin was a hero again when the Soviets won the inaugural 1960 European Championship final. Milan Galic had given Yugoslavia the lead, right winger Slava Metreveli leveled, and journalist turned-center forward Viktor Ponedelnik wrote his own page in history by scoring the extra time winner. The Soviet Union lost the 1964 final 2-1 to Spain and finished fourth in the 1966 World Cup finals.

RIGHT Russia prepare for their Euro 2008 adventure

The change in the balance of power is reflected in the league honors list when the Soviet Union was finally wiped off the map. Kyiv won 13 league titles in the Soviet era, Spartak Moscow 12, Dynamo Moscow 11, CSKA Moscow seven, and Lokomotiv Moscow three.

Yet not once in the Soviet era did a Russian club win a European Cup. That feat had to wait until 2005 when CSKA Moscow beat Sporting Lisbon 3-1 in the UEFA Cup final. Zenit St. Petersburg followed their example in 2008, when they also won the UEFA Cup, beating Rangers. Those achievements demonstrated how far Russian clubs have come since the break up of the Soviet Union and the formation of a Russian league—then virtually bankrupt—in 1992.

The collapse of funding for football clubs from the various state organizations threw the domestic game into turmoil. Within a decade, only

Lokomotiv were still in the controlling hands of the railway unions. All the other clubs had long since been cast adrift by the secret police (Dynamo), army (CSKA), and farms (Spartak).

The domestic game was rescued by the oligarchs who had taken massive financial advantage of the collapse of Communism and the sell-offs of the major utilities. Roman Abramovich's oil company Sibneft originally supported CSKA and the Russian energy giant Gazprom funded the 2007 champions Zenit. The outcome has been that Russian clubs now import star players from all over the world.

But Russian football's growing confidence has been shaken by the national team's failure to qualify for the 2010 World Cup finals. Their play-off defeat by unfancied Slovenia came as a nasty shock after Russia's exciting progress to the Euro 2008 semi-finals.

ABOVE Legendary goalkeeper Lev Yashin defies Portugal's Eusébio at the 1966 World Cup

GREAT NATIONS
REST OF THE WORLD

From small nations such as Luxembourg and San Marino to the array of African sides and former Soviet states, the status and power of world football is forever changing.

ALBANIA (Europe): Despite being among UEFA's founder members in 1954, Albanian football has been hampered by the country's poverty and isolation. They beat newly-crowned European champions Greece in the 2006 World Cup qualifiers, but are still waiting to reach their first tournament—though Albania's star midfielder Lorik Cana has proved outstanding at Marseille.

BELOW Bulgaria's Hristo Stoichkov (left) celebrates another goal for Barcelona

ALGERIA (Africa): Having broken away from France in 1958, Algeria's footballers beat eventual finalists West Germany at the 1982 World Cup thanks to Lakhdar Belloumi's goal but were eliminated in a convenient draw between the West Germans and Austria. Their finest moment came when Moussa Saïb captained the hosts to success at the 1990 African Cup of Nations. JS Kabylie are dominant at home, having won 13 league titles.

ANDORRA (Europe): Not too much can be expected of a country with a population of 72,000, squeezed between Spain and France. Andorra's team, largely made up of part-timers, only began playing international football in 1997. Ce Principat and FC Santa Coloma have won three league titles apiece since 1995.

ANGOLA (Africa): On the rise after years of being constrained by civil war and having their finest players poached by Portugal, Angola made an encouraging World Cup finals debut in 2006. Petro Atlético have been crowned as Angolan champions 13 times.

AUSTRALIA (Asia): After achieving nothing at the 1974 World Cup, the "Socceroos" did not bounce back until 2006, when Dutch manager Guus Hiddink made effective use of such talents as Tim Cahill, Harry Kewell, and Mark Viduka. The nation left the uncompetitive Oceania Football Federation for Asia later that year. The A-League kicked off in 2005–06, with one grand final triumph apiece for Melbourne Victory, Newcastle Jets, and Sydney FC.

AUSTRIA (Europe): The so-called "Wunderteam" of the 1930s, inspired by playmaker Matthias Sindelar and coach Hugo Meisl, finished fourth at the 1934 World Cup. Austrian coach Ernst Happel took Holland to the 1978 World Cup final; the Ernst Happel Stadium in Vienna is named after him. The stadium was also the venue for the Euro 2008 final. Rapid Vienna lead the way in home games, with an astonishing 31 league titles.

AZERBAIJAN (Europe): This former Soviet state has struggled since independence despite a spell in charge by World Cup-winning Brazil captain Carlos Alberto. The main stadium in Baku is named after linesman Tofik Bakhmarov, who decided England's third goal in the 1966 World Cup final really did cross the line. Neftchi Baku have won five league titles.

BELARUS (Europe): Midfielder Alexander Hleb put Belarus on the map with his club displays in Germany and England, but the former Soviet state narrowly missed out on a place at the 2002 World Cup finals after a last-gasp defeat to Wales. Dinamo Minsk have been the dominant side, with seven league crowns to their credit.

BELGIUM (Europe): Despite its small size, Belgium reached the 1980 European Championship final, beat holders Argentina in the opening game of the 1982 World Cup, and finished fourth in 1986 under Guy Thys. Goalkeeper Jean-Marie Pfaff, defender Eric Gerets, midfielder Jan Ceulemans, and forward Enzo Scifo formed the side's spine. Anderlecht have won not only a record 29 league titles but one UEFA Cup, a pair of European Super Cups, twice been crowned European Champions, and twice won the Cup Winners' Cup.

BOLIVIA (South America): The Hernando Siles Stadium in the capital of La Paz is one of the world's highest playing surfaces, at 3,637 meters above sea level. The national side have struggled, although they did win the 1963 Copa America courtesy of a 5-4 win over Brazil. Bolívar FC have won the domestic league 15 times.

BOSNIA-HERZEGOVINA (Europe): This former Yugoslav republic was accepted by UEFA in 1991, but promising players such as midfield schemer Zvjezdan Misimovic have not yet been able to reach a major tournament. Their football association has been under fire for its problems.

BULGARIA (Europe): This is one of Eastern Europe's most consistent producers of quality players. The national team's finest achievement was in reaching the World Cup semi-finals in 1994 with a team starring the legendary Hristo Stoichkov and Emil Kostadinov. The record domestic champions are CSKA Sofia with 31 league titles to their credit.

CAMEROON (Africa): Known as the "Indomitable Lions," they were the surprise package at the 1990 World Cup. They upset holders Argentina and pushed England hard in the quarter-finals, spearheaded by veteran striker Roger Milla. Barcelona's Samuel Eto'o holds the scoring record for the African Cup of Nations, a competition that Cameroon have won four times. Canon Yaoundé have won the African Championship three times to match their 11 domestic league titles.

CANADA (North America): Often over-shadowed by CONCACAF rivals such as Mexico and the US, Canada failed to win the CONCACAF Gold Cup in 1990. This was despite spectacular saves from their former Premiership goalkeeper Craig Forrest and the goalscoring talents of Carlo Corazzin.

CHILE (South America): Strike duo Marcelo Salas and Iván Zamorano helped guide Chile to the 1998 World Cup quarter-finals. But Chile's best run came when hosting the 1962 tournament, when they eventually lost to Brazil in a fiery semi-final. Colo-Colo have won 27 Chilean league titles, more than double the tally of their main rivals.

ABOVE Samuel Eto'o acknowledges the cheers greeting another of his goals for Cameroon

GREAT NATIONS
REST OF THE WORLD

CHINA (Asia): The national team faced Manila in Asia's first international match in 1913, but made their World Cup finals debut only in 2002 when they lost all three matches. Versatile midfielder Zheng Zhi captained the side that hosted but lost the 2004 Asian Cup final to Japan.

COLOMBIA (South America): Carlos Valderrama, Faustino Asprilla and goalkeeper Rene Higuita (famous for his "scorpion kick") made Colombia one of the world's most entertaining sides in the 1990s. Iván Córdoba's goal beat Mexico in the 2001 Copa America final. Club Deportivo Los Millonarios, whose riches lured stars such as Alfredo Di Stefano in the 1940s and 1950s, have picked up 13 league titles.

CONGO DR (Africa): Under their former name of Zaire, they became the first black African side to reach the World Cup finals. But at the 1974 competition they were humiliated by eventual champions West Germany. They were crowned African champions in 1968 and 1974, but government support for the sport has dwindled since then, despite striker Lomana LuaLua's recent Premiership experience. AS Vita Club and DC Motema Pembe each have 11 league titles.

COSTA RICA (Central America): Consistent performers who reached their first World Cup in 1990 under charismatic coach Bora Milutinovic. They also appeared at the 2002 and 2006 tournaments. with striker Paolo Wanchope as the figurehead. They have won nine CONCACAF

championships, though surprisingly none since 1989. Former CONCACAF club champions Deportivo Saprissa have a record 26 domestic league titles.

CROATIA (Europe): This Balkan country taught England a footballing lesson in qualifiers for the 2008 European Championship—just as they did to Germany on their way to third place at the 1998 World Cup. Back then they were inspired by the likes of Robert Prosinecki, Golden Boot winner Davor Šuker, and future national coach Slaven Bilic. More recently, Brazilian-born striker Eduardo and nimble midfielders Luka Modric and Ivan Rakitic have caught the eye. Dinamo Zagred have won the league 11 times since Croatia achieved independence from the former Yugoslavia.

CYPRUS (Europe): Small fry who were thrilled to pull off 1-1 draws against Italy, Czechoslovakia, and France in the 1990s. APOEL Nicosia and Omonia Nicosia have won the Cypriot league 19 times each.

CZECH REPUBLIC (Europe): The Czechs formed the larger part of the old Czechoslovakia, which reached the World Cup Final in 1934 and 1962—when Czech wing half Josef Masopust was voted European Footballer of the Year. Czechoslovakia won the European Championship in 1976. The "new" Czech Republic side lost the Euro 1996 final to Germany on a "golden goal." They also reached the semi-finals of Euro 2004. Sparta Prague have dominated domestic football, winning 11 championships since the Czechs and Slovaks split in 1993. But the best Czech players

ABOVE Colombia's Carlos Valderrama has earned more than 100 caps playing for his country

inevitably move to the big clubs in the West. Pavel Nedved of Juventus was voted European Footballer of the Year in 2003. Other stars have included Petr Cech (Chelsea), Tomas Rosicky (Dortmund and Arsenal), and Champions' Cup-winner Vladimir Smicer (Lens and Liverpool).

DENMARK (Europe): The Danes' greatest triumph came in 1992, when a goal by John Jensen beat Germany 1-0 to win the European Championship final. The Danes also reached the semi-finals of Euro 1984 and the last 16 of the 1986 World Cup. Denmark has produced many stars for rich Western clubs, such as the Laudrup brothers (Michael and Brian), Morten Olsen, and Manchester United great Peter Schmeichel.

ECUADOR (South America): Qualified for the last two World Cup finals tournaments and reached the last 16 in 2006.

EGYPT (Africa): Won the African Cup of Nations for a record sixth time in 2008, beating Cameroon 1-0 in the final.

EL SALVADOR (Central America): Reached the 1970 World Cup finals by beating local rivals Honduras. This stoked up an already tense situation between the two countries, culminating in a six-day conflict that became known as "the football war."

ESTONIA (Europe): Flora Tallinn have dominated the domestic championship since Estonia became a republic in 1992.

FAROE ISLANDS (Europe): The Faroes' best results have been a 1-0 win over Austria and a 2-2 draw with Scotland, both in European Championship qualifiers.

FINLAND (Europe): Noted for producing players for Europe's big clubs, such as Jari Litmanen (Ajax) and Sami Hyypia (Liverpool). The domestic championship has been dominated by HJK Helsinki, United Tampere, and Haka Valkeakoski.

GEORGIA (Europe): Their greatest moment came in 1981, when Dinamo Tbilisi, inspired by midfielder David Kipiani, beat Carl Zeiss Jena 2-1 in the European Cup Winners' Cup final.

GHANA (Africa): Ghana reached the last 16 of the 2006 World Cup finals with a team featuring Premier League stars such as Michael Essien and Sulley Muntari. They have won the African Cup of Nations four times.

ABOVE Theo Zagorakis, a European title-winning hero for Greece

GREAT NATIONS
REST OF THE WORLD

GREECE (Europe): Shock winners of the 2004 European Championship when Otto Rehhagel's side beat hosts Portugal 1-0 in the final with a goal from Angelos Charisteas. They then failed to qualify for the 2006 World Cup finals. Panathinaikos reached the 1971 European Cup final, losing to Ajax at Wembley. Olympiakos have dominated the domestic game, winning 11 of the last 12 championships. In 2008, they became the first Greek side to play in the last 16 of the Champions League.

HAITI (Central/North America): Haiti reached the World Cup finals in 1974 when Emmanuel Sanon scored a historic goal against Italy but have not been back since. They were CONCACAF champions in 1957 and 1973.

HONDURAS (Central/North America): Reaching the World Cup finals for the only time in 1982, they had been CONCACAF champions the previous year.

HUNGARY (Europe): The "Magnificent Magyars" were the finest team in the world in the early 1950s. Led by Ferenc Puskas, they included greats such as striker Sandor Kocsis, playmaker Nandor Hidegkuti, flying winger Zoltan Czibor, goalkeeper Gyula Grocis, and wing half Jozsef Boszik. But they were shocked by West Germany in the 1954 World Cup Final and the team broke up two years later after the Budapest uprising against Soviet control. A new side finished third in the 1964 European Championship and reached the 1966 World Cup quarter-finals after beating Brazil 3-1. Hungary have struggled at international level ever since.

ICELAND (Europe): Yet to make an impact in major competitions, they are, however, well known for exporting star players, such as former Chelsea and Barcelona forward Eidur Gudjohnsen.

INDIA (Asia): The team reached the World Cup finals once, in 1950, but withdrew after FIFA barred them from playing in bare feet.

IRAN (Asia): Although they have reached the World Cup finals three times, they have yet to reach the last 16. They have won the Asian Cup three times. Iran's best player Ali Daei has won 149 caps.

IRAQ (Asia): Iraq are the current Asian Cup holders after beating favorites Saudi Arabia 1-0 in the 2007 final.

ISRAEL (Asia): Israeli clubs dominated the early years of the Asian Club Championship, before political problems forced the country out into the cold and then into UEFA. The national team were World Cup finalists in 1970.

BELOW Haiti's Sanon runs with the ball in a 1974 World Cup match against Italy

LEFT The Ivory Coast team before their game against Ghana in the 2008

IVORY COAST (Africa): Winners of the African Cup of Nations in 1992, the national team reached the World Cup finals for the first time in 2006. The country is most famous for exporting star players such as Didier Drogba and Salomon Kalou (Chelsea), Kolo Toure (Arsenal), and Toure Yaya (Barcelona).

JAMAICA (Central America): Their best performance was reaching the 1998 World Cup finals with a team that included many England-based players.

JAPAN (Asia): Reaching the World Cup finals in 1998, Japan advanced to a best-yet place in the last 16 on home soil in 2002. They have won the Asian Cup three times.

KAZAKHSTAN (Europe): After gaining independence from the Soviet Union, the country switched from the Asian Confederation to UEFA in 2002. Arguably their greatest player was Oleg Litvinenko, who died tragically in November 2007, just four days short of his 34th birthday.

KUWAIT (Asia): The national team had one appearance in the World Cup finals in 1982. They managed a draw with Czechoslovakia but lost to both England and France. During the last of these, France famously "scored" while some of the Kuwaiti players had stopped playing, having heard a whistle. They walked off the pitch in protest and resumed only after the goal was disallowed.

LATVIA (Europe): Having regained their independence in 1991, they are the only Baltic team to have qualified for the European Championship finals when they upset Turkey in the qualifiers.

LIECHTENSTEIN (Europe): One of the whipping boys of European football, comprising mainly part-timers, the tiny principality improved in the Euro 2008 qualifiers when they upset Latvia 1-0 and followed that up with a 3-0 win over Iceland.

LITHUANIA (Europe): They came third in their group in both the Euro 96 and 1998 World Cup qualifying campaigns. Since then they have managed away draws with both Germany and Italy but, like many former Soviet states, they lack depth of quality as yet.

LUXEMBOURG (Europe): Historically one of Europe's minor teams, they once went 12 years without winning a competitive fixture.

ABOVE Mexico's Rafael Marquez and keeper Oswaldo Sanchez clear their lines at the 2006 World Cup

MACEDONIA (Europe): Only since the breakup of Yugoslavia have they had their own officially recognized team. The inaugural Macedonian side featured Darko Pancev, who won the Champions League with Red Star Belgrade in 1991. Away draws with England and Holland represent two of the country's modest high spots.

MALTA (Europe): With one of the oldest national associations in Europe, Malta owes much of its football fanaticism to the island's former British occupation. With a population of under 400,000, however, the national team draws from one of the smallest on the European continent.

MEXICO (Central and North America): Having qualified for no fewer than 13 World Cup finals, Mexico are hugely experienced. They reached the quarter-finals in 1970 and 1986, both times on home soil. Their 2-1 defeat by Argentina in the 2006 World Cup was regarded as one of the finest technical matches of recent tournaments.

MOLDOVA (Europe): Their two best-ever results came within a month of each other in the mid-1990s during the qualifiers for Euro 96, beating Georgia and Wales.

MONTENEGRO (Europe): Came into existence only after the 2006 World Cup after being politically tied to Serbia. The 2010 tournament is their first competitive opportunity.

MOROCCO (Africa): The first African team to win a group at the World Cup (1986), finishing ahead of Portugal, Poland, and England. Although always a contender, they have won the African Nations Cup only once, in 1976. Mustapha

Hadji is arguably their best-known player having starred with both Benfica and Deportivo de La Coruna.

NEW ZEALAND (Oceania): In a country where rugby union is king, the New Zealand football league is semi-professional. They have reached the World Cup finals only once, in 1982, but lost all three games.

NIGERIA (Africa): With a rich footballing pedigree, Nigeria has exported a string of exceptional players to Europe. Current squad members include Obefemi Martins and Mikel John Obi. The "Super Eagles" usually reach the World Cup finals though they missed out in 2006 when Angola qualified instead.

NORTHERN IRELAND (Europe): Fans still talk nostalgically about their heyday when they qualified for the 1982 World Cup, reaching the quarter-finals, having beaten hosts Spain. Norman Whiteside became the youngest-ever player in the finals, at 17 years 41 days. Billy Bingham, a player in the team who had also reached the quarter-finals in 1958, was the manager and led his country to the finals again in 1986, the smallest European nation to qualify twice.

NORTH KOREA (Asia): The North Koreans' shining moment came in the 1966 World Cup when they upset Italy 1-0 to gain a spot in the quarter-finals. There, they went 3-0 up against Portugal, but the brilliance of Eusébio and his four goals stopped the fairytale and the match ended with the Koreans down 5-3. They have never threatened a repeat; political isolation has cost their football dear.

NORWAY (Europe): The greatest moment in Norwegian football, a 2-1 win over Brazil in the 1998 World Cup, sparked wild scenes back home. Rosenborg, the country's leading club, have perennially competed in the Champions League but almost all of Norway's top players go abroad even though the domestic league is now professional.

PARAGUAY (South America): Although they reached the second round of the World Cup in 1986, 1998, and 2002, they have never advanced beyond that stage. They Won the Copa América 1953 and 1979.

PERU (South America): Peru's "golden generation" in the 1970s and early 1980s was highlighted by the skills of Teofilo Cubillas, who scored five goals in two different World Cup finals. Defender Hector Chumputaz was one of the first South American players to have one hundred international appearances.

POLAND (Europe): They have twice finished third in the World Cup in 1974 and 1982, thanks to talents of outstanding players such as Zbigniew Boniek and Grzegorz Lato. Goalkeeper Jan Tomaszewski, whose performance at Wembley in 1973 prevented England reaching the World Cup finals in West Germany, remains an icon..

QATAR (Asia): Opening up the domestic league to foreign players turned Qatar into an attractive and lucrative new destination for veteran stars. But Qatar's wealth has also been invested in a sports academy to help develop home-grown talent.

REPUBLIC OF IRELAND (Europe): The Irish enjoyed their most euphoric era under the guidance of Jack Charlton and his successor Mick McCarthy. They qualified for Euro 88, reaching the quarter-finals of the 1990 World Cup and making the last

16 at both the 1994 and 2002 World Cups. The side gets its strength from the fact that most of the squad star in the English Premier League.

ROMANIA (Europe): The national side contested the first World Cup in 1930, and their "golden generation," led by Gheorghe Hagi, reached the 1994 World Cup quarter-finals. Steaua Bucharest became the first Eastern European side to win the European Champions Cup in 1985. The domestic scene is dominated by the clubs from Bucharest, with Steaua and Dinamo holding 41 titles between them.

SAUDI ARABIA (Asia): Three-time Asian Cup champions, their former goalkeeper Mohamed Al-Deayea is the most capped international male footballer, with 181 appearances. Al-Hilal have won the league title 11 times since it began in 1972.

SCOTLAND (Europe): The first-ever international game took place between Scotland and England in 1872. The fixture remains one of football's fiercest rivalries. Scotland have never reached the second stage of an international tournament, despite a famous victory over the Netherlands in 1978. The "Old Firm," Celtic and Rangers, enjoy a near-monopoly on the Scottish Premier League Championship. In 1967, Celtic became the first British team to win the European Champions Cup. Scottish players and managers have contributed enormously to the English League, including Kenny Daglish and Graeme Sounness at Liverpool and Sir Alex Ferguson at Manchester United.

SENEGAL (Africa): This nation's team stunned the world by beating defending title-holders France in the 2002 World Cup on their way to becoming only the second African team to reach the tournament's quarter-finals.

ABOVE Kenny Dalglish, hero of Scotland and Celtic

REST OF THE WORLD

SERBIA (Europe): They became a single footballing nation in 2006 after Montenegro gained independence. Serbia's most powerful clubs remain the ones that dominated within the original Yugoslavia—Partizan and Red Star, both from Belgrade.

SLOVAKIA (Europe): Originally a member of FIFA in 1907, Slovakia rejoined in 1994 after the break-up of Czechoslovakia. But they have yet to qualify for an international tournament's final stages.

SLOVENIA (Europe): A decade after gaining independence from Yugoslavia, Slovenia reached its first finals in the 2000 European Championship and the 2002 World Cup. NK Maribor, which beat Villarreal to win the 2006 Intertoto Cup, hold the most Slovenian league titles, with seven.

SOUTH AFRICA (Africa): They will become the first African nation to host the World Cup finals in 2010. Re-admitted to world footballing bodies in 1990 after the end of apartheid, the national team won the African Cup of Nations in 1996 after stepping in at the last minute as hosts. South African players Benni McCarthy, Mark Fish, Lucas Radebe, and Quinton Fortune have been successful at European club level.

SOUTH KOREA (Asia): With their semi-final appearance in 2002, South Korea recorded the best-ever performance by an Asian team in the World Cup. Traditionally strong in Asia, they won the first two Asian Cups. Manchester United's Park Ji-Sung is the most famous South Korean player in the world. Seongnam Ilhwa Chunma are the K-League's most successful team with seven championship trophies. Korean clubs have won the Asian Champions Cup seven times since 1985.

SWEDEN (Europe): World Cup runners-up as hosts in 1958, Sweden have also reached three other semi-finals, the most recent being third place in 1994. Swedish players have been successful across Europe, and Swede Sven-Göran Eriksson won the Italian title at Lazio before managing England to three successive quarter-finals. IFK Gothenburg are the leading domestic title-winners with 18, just ahead of Malmö on 15. IFK are also the only Swedish club to have won a European trophy, twice landing the UEFA Cup.

SWITZERLAND (Europe): One of Switzerland's major roles in the world game is off the pitch—hosting FIFA headquarters in Zurich and UEFA's headquarters near Geneva. Switzerland holds the dubious honor of being the only team to be eliminated from the World Cup (in 2006) in a penalty shoot-out without netting a single spot-kick. The domestic league is dominated by Grasshopper Club (27 titles) and the recently resurgent FC Zurich and FC Basel.

TOGO (Africa): Togo's first-ever appearance in the World Cup in 2006 was blighted by a dispute over player bonuses. The federation was subsequently fined by FIFA for "behavior unworthy of a participant in the World Cup." Tragedy struck in 2007, when 20 members of their delegation to the African Cup of Nations qualifier, including the Sports Minister but not any players, were killed in a helicopter crash. They have never gone past the first stage of the African Cup of Nations.

BELOW Trinidad's Dwight Yorke strikes for goal against Paraguay

TRINIDAD AND TOBAGO (Central and North America): Ex-Manchester United striker Dwight Yorke is such a hero in Tobago that the national stadium bears his name. Other notable players to have succeeded in England include goalkeeper Shaka Hislop, Stern John, and Kenwyne Jones. Trinidad and Tobago qualified for their first World Cup in 2006, where they were eliminated without scoring a goal.

TURKEY (Europe): Turkey's biggest footballing success came in the 2002 World Cup, where they finished third. Turkish teams have proved fearsome opposition in the UEFA Champions League, especially in their home legs, where an intimidating atmosphere is guaranteed. Hakan Sukur, scorer of the fastest-ever World Cup goal in 11 seconds in 2006, is Turkish football's top scorer. Only four clubs have won the Turkish top flight since 1959—Fenerbahce and Galatasaray (17 each), Besiktas (11), and Trabzonspor (six).

TUNISIA (Africa): Tunisia were the first African team to win a World Cup finals match, beating Mexico 3-1. They won the African Cup of Nations as host in 2004.

UKRAINE (Europe): Having provided some of the finest players to the Soviet Union national team for years, Ukraine reached the quarter-finals in their first World Cup as an independent nation, in 2006. Dynamo Kiev, the most successful Ukrainian team with 12 championships, were often the only challenger to Moscow clubs' domination during the Soviet era. Andriy Shevchenko and Sergei Rebrov spearheaded their European campaigns in the mid–late 1990s before the latter moved on to great success in Italy with AC Milan.

UNITED ARAB EMIRATES (Asia): The UAE has a lively and popular domestic league, dominated by Al-Ain FC, the first UAE winners of the Asian Champions Cup, in 2003. The

national team's only appearance at a World Cup in 1990 ended in three defeats. Their one major international success was in winning the 2007 Gulf Cup of Nations.

UNITED STATES OF AMERICA (Central and North America): Though football struggles to compete with other American sports, the game is hugely popular with both young men and women. The US women's team are one of the most successful in the world, having won the inaugural Women's World Cup in 1991 and repeated the feat in 1999, thanks to key players such as Brandi Chastain and Mia Hamm. The men's professional domestic league, the MLS, has attracted European stars such as David Beckham.

URUGUAY (South America): The first hosts and first winners of the World Cup in 1930, Uruguay won the tournament again in 1950, but are no longer the international force they once were. Peñarol (36) and Nacional (30) have won the most national championships.

VENEZUELA (South America): Venezuela are the only member of the South American federation never to have qualified for the World Cup finals. Their best performance in the Copa America came when they reached the quarter-finals as hosts in 2007.

WALES (Europe): Few Welsh teams play in the English Football League. Cardiff City are the only non-English side to ever win the English FA Cup (in 1927) and they were runners-up to Portsmouth in 2008. Wales reached their only World Cup finals in 1958, with "Gentle Giant" John Carles, leading them to a quarter-final defeat against Brazil. Despite producing word-famous players in the 1980s and 1990s, they have failed to qualify for an international tournament since then.

ABOVE David Beckham turns on the style in the US for LA Galaxy

GREAT CLUBS

Club football provides the power base that keeps supporters mesmerized across the world, week-in and week-out. Initially, domestic leagues and cup competitions provided the staple diet for fans, but then the glamor of international competition provided icing on the cake from the 1950s onwards. Nowadays, international competition is crucial to the financial health of many clubs, and provides the funds that keep fans entertained with high-profile new signings.

GREAT CLUBS
EUROPE

AJAX AMSTERDAM (Holland)

Ajax reached their peak in the early 1970s, when they pioneered the style known as "Total Football" and won the European Cup three times in a row. Coach Rinus Michels painstakingly built the side, led by the legendary Johan Cruyff, for five years before their victories from 1971 to 1973. Cruyff was the coach when Ajax lifted their next European trophy, the Cup Winners' Cup, in 1987. The club's renowned youth system produced another European Cup-winning side in 1995, which finished as runner-up the following season. But the effects of the "Bosman Rule" have diminished Ajax's power, and now their stars inevitably move to richer clubs abroad.

Titles: Club World Cup 1972, 1995; European Cup 1971, 1972, 1973, 1995; UEFA Cup 1992; European Cup Winners' Cup 1987; Dutch champions 29 times; Dutch cup 18

ARSENAL (England)

Arsenal became the dominant force in England in the 1930s. Manager Herbert Chapman created their first truly great side, which won four league titles in five seasons, including three in a row between 1933 and 1935. After two post-war titles, Arsenal went through a barren spell. Victory over Anderlecht in the 1970 Fairs Cup final brought their first trophy for 17 years. They won the domestic double the following season and star player George Graham later delivered two more titles as coach with a host of home-grown players. Long-serving manager Arsène Wenger imported a number of foreign players with a French connection. His rewards include two league and cup doubles.

Titles: UEFA/Fairs Cup 1970; European Cup Winners' Cup: 1994; English champions 13 times; FA Cup 10; League Cup 2

ASTON VILLA (England)

Aston Villa were one of the 12 founding members of the Football League in 1888. They were a major force in its early years, winning five championships between 1894 and 1900 and the double in 1897. But after lifting the FA Cup in 1920, they went 37 years before gaining another major honor, beating Manchester United in the FA Cup final. Their most remarkable success was winning the European Cup in 1982. A quarter-final defeat by Juventus in 1983 signaled the start of a decline, and they were relegated in 1987. Aston Villa regained their elite status a season later. They finished league runner-up in both the 1989–90 and 1992–93 seasons.

Titles: European Cup 1982; English champions 7 times; FA Cup 7; League Cup 5

ATLETICO MADRID (Spain)

Atletico have spent years playing second fiddle to Real Madrid, although they overshadowed their neighbors in the early 1950s, when coach Helenio Herrera guided them to successive titles. Spanish champions in 1973, they came within a minute of winning the European Cup a year later. They were denied glory by a late equalizer that forced a replay, which Bayern Munich won 4-0. Atletico won the 1974 Club World Cup after Bayern declined to compete. The club became synonymous with instability under president Jesus Gil, who hired and fired 23 different coaches between 1987 and 2003. They revived under Mexican coach Javier Aguirre, and in 2008 secured entry into the European Champions League. Two years later, they became the first winners of the Europa League, defeating English side Fulham 2-1 in the final.

Titles: Intercontinental Cup 1974; European Cup Winners' Cup 1962; Europa League 2010; Spanish champions 9 times; Spanish cup 9

BARCELONA (Spain)

Barcelona's motto is "More than a Club," and they have long been a symbol for Catalonia's regional pride. Their bitter rivalry with Real Madrid is a key feature of Spanish football. Barcelona, coached by former great Pep Guardiola, have outshone Madrid completely in the past two seasons, winning the Champions League, Spanish league and cup treble in 2009 and adding another domestic championship in 2010. Ronald Koeman's European Cup final winner against Sampdoria in 1992 had earlier healed Barcelona's wounded pride after so many disappointments in the competition, including defeats in the final to Benfica and Steaua Bucharest. Coach Johan Cruyff created the winning "Dream Team," featuring Koeman, Guardiola, Hristo Stoichkov, and Michael Laudrup—which many regard as Barcelona's best-ever team. Frank Rijkaard, Cruyff's protege, later crafted the 2005–06 side that beat Arsenal 2-1 in the Champions League final and won La Liga.

Titles: European Cup 1992, 2006, 2009; UEFA/Fairs Cup 1958, 1960, 1966; European Cup Winners' Cup 1979, 1982, 1989, 1997; Spanish champions 20 times; Spanish cup 25

BAYERN MUNICH (Germany)

Bayern Munich succeeded Ajax as the dominant team in Europe in the mid-1970s, winning the European Cup three times in a row. The great Franz Beckenbauer was their conductor, supported by prolific striker Gerd Müller, and goalkeeper Sepp Maier. But Bayern came within a minute of losing the 1974 final to Atletico Madrid, before leveling and winning the replay 4-0. A year later they beat Leeds United 2-0 and completed their trio with a 1-0 win over Saint-Etienne. Bayern added a fourth European Cup triumph in 2001, when goalkeeper Oliver Kahn defied Valencia in a penalty shoot-out. They have appeared in eight finals, the latest their 2010 defeat by Internazionale. At home, they have dominated the Bundesliga, winning 22 championships to add to their all-German title of 1932.

Titles: Intercontinental Cup 1976, 2001; European Cup 1974, 1975, 1976, 2001; European Cup Winners' Cup 1967; UEFA Cup 1996; German champions 22 times; German cup 15

BENFICA (Portugal)

Benfica fans look back on the 1960s as their club's golden years. They succeeded Real Madrid as European champions by beating Barcelona 3-2 in the 1961 final, then retained the European Cup with a 5-3 win over Real Madrid. Benfica also reached the final in 1963, 1965, and 1968 and supplied the bulk of the Portugal side that finished third in the 1966 World Cup finals. Benfica's hero was the great striker Eusébio. The team was packed with internationals, with Mario Coluna pulling the strings in midfield. Benfica lost in recent finals to PSV Eindhoven, on penalties in 1988, and AC Milan in 1990. They won a record 32nd domestic championship in 2010 under new coach Jorge Jesus.

Titles: European Cup 1961, 1962; Portuguese champions 32 times; Portuguese cup 24

BELOW Henrik Larsson, Carles Puyol and Ronaldinho take the Champions League Cup by tickertape storm in 2006

GREAT CLUBS
EUROPE

BORUSSIA DORTMUND (Germany)

Borussia Dortmund became the first West German team to lift a European trophy after they beat Liverpool in the 1966 Cup Winners' Cup final. But their greatest day came in 1997, when Ottmar Hitzfeld's side stunned Juventus 3-1 in the Champions League final. Hitzfeld had brought back Matthias Sammer, Andy Möller, Jürgen Koller, and Stefan Reuter from Italy to form the core of the team. Five years later, Borussia Dortmund won the Bundesliga and reached the UEFA Cup final, losing to Feyenoord. They came perilously close to bankruptcy in 2005.

Titles: Intercontinental Cup 1997; European Cup 1997; European Cup Winners' Cup 1966; German champions 6 times; German cup 2

CELTIC (Scotland)

Celtic were the first British club to win the European Cup when they beat Internazionale 2-1 in the 1967 final in Lisbon. The team were known as the "Lisbon Lions," and were all born within a 30-mile radius of Glasgow. Celtic also reached the final in 1970. They were managed by Jock Stein, and included outstanding figures such as Tommy Gemmell, Billy McNeill, Bobby Murdoch, and Jimmy Johnstone. That team began to break up after losing the 1974 European Cup semi-final to Atletico Madrid. But they still set a domestic record of nine consecutive championships. Celtic revived memories of those glory days with a run to the 2003 UEFA Cup final. Their fierce rivalry with Rangers still dominates Scottish football.

Titles: European Cup 1967; Scottish champions 42 times; Scottish Cup 31; League Cup 14

CHELSEA (England)

Chelsea's recent transformation into a European power has been bankrolled by Russian oil billionaire Roman Abramovich, the club's owner since 2003. His appointment of Portugal's Jose Mourinho as manager a year later galvanized the club. Mourinho spent heavily to win the Premier League and the League Cup, and delivered another league title in 2006. He left Chelsea in September 2007, despite guiding them to FA Cup and League Cup victories, after falling out with Abramovich. Israeli Avram Grant then took Chelsea to their first Champions League final, but was sacked after their shoot-out defeat by Manchester United. In 2010, incoming coach Carlo Ancelotti steered Chelsea to their first-ever double of Premier League and FA Cup. They also scored a record 103 Premiership goals.

Titles: European Cup Winners' Cup 1971, 1998; English champions 4 times; FA Cup 6; League Cup 4

DYNAMO KYIV (Ukraine)

Dynamo Kyiv were the first club from the former Soviet Union to win a European trophy when they beat Hungary's Ferencváros in the 1975 European Cup Winners' Cup final. They saw off Atletico Madrid 3-0 to win the same competition 11 years later. The Ukrainians led non-Russian opposition to the Moscow clubs during the Soviet era, winning 13 championships and nine cup finals. They are seasoned UEFA Champions League competitors, despite normally starting in the qualifying stages, and reached the semi-final stage in 1999. Andriy Shevchenko was their inspiration with eight goals, earning him a lucrative move to AC Milan.

Titles: UEFA Cup Winners Cup 1975, 1986; Soviet champions 13 times; Ukrainian champions 12 times; Soviet cup 9; Ukrainian cup 9

BELOW Barcelona's Thierry Henry fails to breach Celtic's defense

EVERTON (England)

Everton, formed in 1878, were founder members of the Football League, and one of its most successful clubs for many years. They reached their peak under Howard Kendall in the mid-1980s. They won the FA Cup in 1984, the league title (ahead of their great rivals, Liverpool) and the Cup Winners' Cup a year later, and added another title in 1987. In between, they finished as runner-up to Liverpool in the league and FA Cup. However, the ban on English clubs after the Heysel Stadium disaster denied Everton the chance to build on their European success, and eventually the team broke up. A string of managers struggled to rebuild in the years that followed, before David Moyes steered Everton to a Champions League qualifying place in 2005. The 1-0 win over Manchester United in the 1995 FA Cup final remains their last major honor.

Titles: European Cup Winners' Cup 1985; English champions 9 times; FA Cup 5

FEYENOORD (Holland)

Feyenoord, from Rotterdam, became the first Dutch team to win the European Cup when they beat Celtic 2-1 after extra time in 1970 in Milan. Four years later, they lifted the UEFA Cup after drawing with Tottenham in the first leg in London and winning the return 2-0. Three of that victorious side, Wim Rijsbergen, Wim Jansen, and Wim Van Hanegem, played for Holland in the 1974 World Cup final. Following almost 20 years without further European success, Feyenoord were surprise UEFA Cup winners in 2002, beating Borussia Dortmund 3-2. They have failed to make any impact in Europe since, and have not won the Dutch title since 1999. Instead, they have become a supplier of stars, including talents such as Robin van Persie, Dirk Kuyt, Salomon Kalou, and Royston Drenthe to clubs in richer leagues.

Titles: Intercontinental Cup 1970; European Cup 1970; UEFA Cup 1974, 2002; Dutch champions 14 times; Dutch cup 11

INTERNAZIONALE (Italy)

Internazionale's 2010 Champions League final victory over Bayern Munich revived memories of their world power in the mid-1960s. They defeated Real Madrid 3-1 in the 1964 European Cup final and beat Benfica 1-0 a year later. But they lost the 1967 final against Celtic. However, coach Helenio Herrera was criticized for his defensive tactics and they were an unpopular side, despite fielding greats such as full back Giacinto Facchetti, midfielder Luis Suarez, and attacker Sandro Mazzola. Internazionale reached another European Cup final in 1972, when they were swept aside by Ajax. After several decades playing second fiddle to AC Milan, they have revived in recent years. They have won each of the last five Italian championships—and, guided by coach Jose Mourinho—they lifted the European Cup for a third time.

Titles: Intercontinental Cup 1964, 1965; European Cup 1964, 1965, 2010; UEFA Cup 1991, 1994, 1998; Italian champions 18 times; Italian cup 6

JUVENTUS (Italy)

Juventus boast an enviable record of appearing in seven European Cup finals. The tragedy of the Heysel Stadium disaster dwarfed their first success, when Michel Platini's goal edged out Liverpool in the 1985 final. They won again in 1996, when Marcello Lippi's team beat Ajax Amsterdam on penalty kicks. Juventus have also lost finals to Ajax, Hamburg SV, Borussia Dortmund, Real Madrid, and AC Milan. They have amassed a record number of Italian titles, but recent successes have been dogged by controversy. Their three title wins between 1995 and 1998 were the subject of a doping enquiry. In 2006, Juventus were stripped of their 2005 and 2006 Serie A titles following a match-fixing scandal. The punishment included relegation, sending them to Serie B for the first time. Despite a 30-point deduction, they won promotion.

Titles: Intercontinental Cup 1985, 1996; European Cup 1985, 1996; European Cup Winners' Cup 1984; UEFA/Fairs Cup 1977, 1990, 1993; Italian champions 27 times; Italian cup 9

ABOVE Alessandro Del Piero of Juventus celebrates a goal against Celtic in 2001

ABOVE Liverpool captain Steven Gerrard lifts the 2005 European Cup in Istanbul

LIVERPOOL (England)

Liverpool are the most successful English club in European competitions. They have won the European Cup five times, the UEFA Cup three times, and have a hat-trick of European Super Cup prizes. Liverpool reached two other European Cup finals and may well have added more appearances to the list, but for the ban imposed on English clubs after the Heysel Stadium disaster. Liverpool changed their style in Europe after a home defeat by Red Star Belgrade and swiftly reaped the rewards from a more patient approach. Bob Paisley, who succeeded Bill Shankly, was the architect of their success. He steered Liverpool to a hat-trick of triumphs in the European Cup—1977, 1978, and 1981—before handing over to Joe Fagan for their 1984 triumph. The Steven Gerrard-inspired comeback known as "the Miracle of Istanbul" brought Liverpool their fifth European Cup in 2005. Paisley's team dominated in England as well as Europe. Such stars as Kenny Dalglish, Alan Hansen, Ian Rush, Graeme Souness, and Phil Thompson helped Liverpool to win a total of 18 championships—an English record. They have not won the league since 1990, and ending that run has become the club's priority.

Titles: European Cup 1977, 1978, 1981, 1984, 2005; UEFA Cup 1973, 1976, 2001; European Super Cup 1977, 2001, 2005; English champions 18 times; FA Cup 7; League Cup 7

LYON (France)

Lyon monopolized French football between 2002 and 2008, when they won seven consecutive championships, a domestic record. In 2008, coached by Alain Perrin, they completed a league and cup double. The 2002 title was Lyon's first, and a realization of the dreams of Jean-Michel Aulas, club president since 1987. Aulas, a computer software millionaire, then set his sights on an even bigger prize: the Champions League. He has employed a succession of top French coaches—Jacques Santini, Paul Le Guen, Gerard Houllier and Perrin —who all delivered championships but never advanced beyond the quarter-finals. Lyon's run to the 2010 Champions League semi-finals under Claude Puel was their best in a major European competition, though they did win the Intertoto Cup in 1997. One of their biggest problems is that they keep losing key players to UEFA Champions League rivals, such as Michael Essien to Chelsea and Mohamadou Diarra and star striker Karim Benzema to Real Madrid.

Titles: Intertoto Cup 1997; French champions 7 times; French cup 4; League cup 1

MANCHESTER CITY (England)

Manchester City have become one of the world's wealthiest clubs, thanks to the massive investment of Abu Dhabi oil magnate Sheikh Mansour bin Nayed. They missed out on a Premier League top four finish by one place in 2009–10 despite spending nearly £200million over the past two years. But life has never been dull at City. Their recent history has seen them suffer the indignity of dropping into the second division before climbing back to the Premier League. Kevin Keegan, Stuart Pearce, Sven-Göran Eriksson, Mark Hughes, and Roberto Mancini have all been in charge since their return to the big time. But City were at their best in the late 1960s. Manager Joe Mercer and assistant Malcolm Allison guided them to the championship in 1968, the FA Cup in 1969 and

the European Cup Winners' Cup and League
Cup the next season.

Titles: European Cup Winners' Cup 1970;
English champions 2; FA Cup 4; League Cup 2

MANCHESTER UNITED (England)

Scottish managers have crafted Manchester
United's post-war achievements. Sir Matt Busby
built the team known as "the Busby Babes"
who won two championships and reached the
European Cup semi-finals twice, before being
torn apart by the Munich air disaster in 1958.
Busby went on to create another great side—
featuring Bobby Charlton, Denis Law, and George
Best—that won two more championships. They
became the first English team to lift the European
Cup, ten years after Munich. Sir Alex Ferguson
then achieved greatness in his own style after
delivering Manchester United's first league title
for 26 years in 1993. His sides have dominated
the Premier League era, claiming 11 of the 18
titles and United have now joined Liverpool on
18 domestic championships. They have also added
two Champions League triumphs—in 1999 and
2008—and lost the 2009 final to Barcelona.
Manchester United's astonishing late rally, capped
by Ole Gunnar Solskjaer's winner, pipped Bayern
Munich in the 1999 final and gave the club a
unique treble, adding to the prizes of the Premier
League and FA Cup. Nine years later, United
keeper Edwin van der Sar held his nerve to
decide the final shoot-out against Chelsea.

Titles: Intercontinental Cup 1999; European
Cup 1968, 1999, 2008; European Cup Winners'
Cup 1991; English champions 18 times; FA Cup
11; League Cup 4

AC MILAN (Italy)

AC Milan come second only to Real Madrid in
terms of European Cup success, having captured
the prize seven times and appeared in four other

finals. They first lifted it in 1963 by deposing
holders Benfica 2-1, and six years later crushed
Ajax Amsterdam 4-1. They had to wait 20 years
for their next victory, when the Dutch trio of
Ruud Gullit, Frank Rijkaard, and Marco Van Basten
inspired Arrigo Sacchi's cultured side to a 4-0 win
over Steaua Bucharest. Milan triumphed again in
1994, tearing Barcelona apart 4-0. Defeat by Ajax
Amsterdam the following year signaled the end
of an era. The Dutchmen had already gone, but
two defenders remained who would star in the
next decade—Alessandro Costacurta and Paolo
Maldini. Milan edged past Juventus on penalty kicks
in 2003, then lost one of the most dramatic finals
in 2005. They led Liverpool 3-0 but were defeated
on penalty kicks. They gained revenge on Liverpool
two years later, when they won 2-1 and Maldini
collected his fifth European Cup winner's medal.

Titles: Intercontinental Cup 1969, 1989, 1990,
2007; European Cup 1963, 1969, 1989, 1990, 1994,
2003, 2007; European Cup Winners' Cup 1968,
1973; Italian champions 17 times; Italian cup 5

ABOVE Andrea Pirlo of
AC Milan takes a free kick
against Atalanta in 2008

AC Milan striker Filippo Inzaghi beats Liverpool goalkeeper Pepe Reina to score his second goal in his team's 2-0 win in the 2007 Champions League final

1960s

1970s

GREAT CLUBS MOMENTS

ABOVE Tottenham's Jimmy Greaves shoots for goal against Burnley

ABOVE Zico (left) is a legendary figure for Flamengo and Brazil

LEFT Benfica's Portugal hero Eusébio bears down on goal

BELOW Celtic keeper Ronnie Simpson defies Internazionale in Lisbon

BELOW Manchester United parade the Champions Cup in 1968

1980s 2000s

ABOVE Hugo Sanchez top-scored for Mexico, Real and Atletico Madrid

BELOW Alex (Santos) tackles Boca's Carlos Tevez

BELOW Carles Pujol and Ronaldinho raise the Champions Cup

RIGHT David Beckham takes to the wing for LA Galaxy

ABOVE Milan forward Kaka eludes Inter's Nelson Rivas

ABOVE RIGHT Etoile Sahel carry off the African Super Cup

GREAT CLUBS
EUROPE

OLYMPIQUE MARSEILLE (France)

Olympique Marseille's greatest achievement also led to their greatest crisis. They became the only French team to have won the European Cup, when they saw off AC Milan in the 1993 final. But Valenciennes midfielder Jacques Glassmann alleged that Marseille's Jean-Jacques Eydelie had tried to bribe him and two other players to "go easy on them" in Marseille's last game before the final. The bribe attempt was traced back to Marseille's managing director Jean-Pierre Bernes and then to club president Bernard Tapie, who was jailed for his involvement. Marseille, who had won the previous five championships, were stripped of their 1993 crown and relegated to the second division. UEFA disqualified them from defending their title. They recovered to reach the UEFA Cup final in 1999 and 2004 and were crowned French champions in 2010 when they also won the League Cup.

Titles: European Cup 1993; French champions 9 times; French cup 10; League cup 1

PORTO (Portugal)

Porto tasted glory under Jose Mourinho, as the new century unfolded. He steered them to the championship and a 2003 UEFA Cup final victory over Celtic. A year later, they were crowned champions of both Portugal and Europe. Mourinho's team destroyed AS Monaco 3-0 in the Champions League final, to deliver Porto's second European Cup triumph. Mourinho then left for Chelsea, taking defensive duo Paulo Ferreira and Ricardo Carvalho with him. Porto have not advanced beyond the last 16 since. But they won the domestic league and cup double in 2009, lifting their sixth title in seven seasons.

Titles: Intercontinental Cup 1987, 2004; European Cup 1987, 2004; UEFA Cup 2003; Portuguese champions 24 times; Portuguese cup 19

PSV EINDHOVEN (Holland)

PSV have overtaken Holland's former elite, Ajax Amsterdam and Feyenoord. They broke the dominance of the "Big Two" in the 1970s, when they won three championships in four seasons. They also snatched the UEFA Cup in 1978 with a 3-0 aggregate win over Bastia. PSV's greatest moment came ten years later, when they beat Benfica on penalties in the European Cup final. The side have continued to challenge in the UEFA Champions League despite losing stars to England, Germany, and Spain. They lost on away goals to AC Milan in the 2005 semi-finals and reached the quarter-finals two years later.

Titles: European Cup 1988; UEFA Cup 1978; Dutch champions 21 times; Dutch cup 8

RANGERS (Scotland)

Rangers' run to the 2008 UEFA Cup final, which they lost 2-0 to Zenit St Petersburg, marked the

BELOW Jorge Costa and Vitor Baia lead Porto's European victory parade in 2004

end of a 36-year gap since their last appearance in a European showpiece. In their previous final, they beat Dynamo Moscow 3-2 to lift the Cup Winners' Cup—their only European prize. In 1961, Rangers lost the first European Cup Winners' Cup final to Fiorentina. A year earlier, they had reached the European Cup semi-finals, but crashed 12-4 on aggregate to Eintracht Frankfurt. They made their biggest impact on the Champions League in 1993, when they finished a point behind winners Marseille in the last eight group stage. Rangers have won a record 53 Scottish League titles.
Titles: European Cup Winners' Cup 1972; Scottish champions 53 times; Scottish Cup 33; League Cup 26

REAL MADRID (Spain)

Real Madrid are the best known club in the world. They won each of the first five finals of the European Cup—defeating Reims twice, Fiorentina, AC Milan, and Eintracht Frankfurt. The club was guided by visionary president Santiago Bernabeu, with the team ably led by the legendary Argentinean center forward Alfredo Di Stefano—who played in all five finals. The most renowned final was the 7-3 victory over Frankfurt in 1960, when Di Stefano hit a hat-trick and Hungary great Ferenc Puskás netted four goals. Winger Paco Gento was the only attacking link with that golden past when Real Madrid's new-look team edged Partizan Belgrade 2-1 to win the trophy again, six years later. They had to wait until 1998 for their next success, when Predrag Mijatovic scored the clincher against Juventus. Vicente Del Bosque revived past glories, steering Real Madrid to Champions League victories in 2000 and 2002. He was sacked after their 2003 semi-final, and club president Florentino Perez put together a star-studded side with the top players known as "Galacticos." Since Del Bosque's departure, Real Madrid have reached the quarter-final stage just once.
Titles: Intercontinental Cup 1960, 1998, 2002; European Cup 1956, 1957, 1958, 1959, 1960, 1966,

1998, 2000, 2002; UEFA Cup 1985, 1986; Spanish champions 31 times; Spanish cup 17

AS ROMA (Italy)

AS Roma have enjoyed their most successful decade recently. They won Serie A in 2001 and have finished runner-up six times in the past nine years, including second place in 2010. They also reached the Champions League quarter-finals in 2007 and 2008. The fulcrum of Roma's success has been Francesco Totti, who holds the club records for games and goals.
Titles: UEFA/Fairs Cup 1961; Italian champions 3 times; Italian cup 9

TOTTENHAM HOTSPUR (England)

Tottenham Hotspur became the first English club to win a European trophy when they beat Atletico Madrid 5-1 in the 1963 European Cup Winners' Cup final. The team are considered Tottenham's best ever. They won the first league and cup double of the 20th century in 1961, collecting the FA Cup again the following season, and reaching the European Cup semi-final. Tottenham have since added two UEFA Cup victories. They finally gained access to the Champions League for the first time in 2010–11.
Titles: European Cup Winners' Cup 1963; UEFA Cup 1972, 1984; English champions 2; FA Cup 8; League Cup 4

BELOW Tottenham Hotspurs' double-winning players enjoy their open-top bus parade in 1961

ABOVE Juan Román Riquelme, a latter-day hero for Boca Juniors

BOCA JUNIORS (Argentina)

No South American club has won more international titles than the Argentine team from La Bombonera, the Buenos Aires stadium whose affectionate nickname translates as "The Chocolate Box." Their "Superclásico" rivalry with River Plate is one of the fiercest in the world, with Boca Juniors' supporters considering themselves as the city's working-class underdogs. Diego Maradona spent a title-winning season with the club before leaving for Spain in 1982, coming back 13 years later. Juan Román Riquelme was a modern-day heir whose return for a second spell led to Copa Libertadores glory in 2007.

Titles: Intercontinental Cup 1977, 2000, 2003; Copa Libertadores 1977, 1978, 2000, 2001, 2003, 2007; Copa Sudamericana 2004, 2005; Argentine league 24 times

COLO COLO (Chile)

The "Snow Whites" of Santiago became the first, and so far only, Chilean club to win the Copa Libertadores—the South American equivalent of the European Cup—in 1991 when they beat Paraguay's Olimpia Asuncion 3-0 on aggregate. They are Chile's most successful club, with 39 domestic trophies and the only club never to have been relegated since the league was founded in 1933.

Titles: Copa Libertadores 1991; Chilean league 29 times; Chilean cup 10

FLAMENGO (Brazil)

Flamengo began life in 1895 as a rowing club but embraced football 16 years later, after a breakaway by aggrieved members of neighboring Fluminense. They have since become Brazil's best-loved club,

with an estimated fanbase of 40 million. However, it was not until the late 1970s and early 1980s that they extended their domestic brilliance to the international arena. Zico was voted Man of the Match as Flamengo trounced Liverpool 3-0 in the 1981 Intercontinental Cup.

Titles: Intercontinental Cup 1981; Copa Libertadores 1981; Brazilian league 6 times; Brazilian cup 2

INDEPENDIENTE (Argentina)

Years of decline and debts forced Independiente to sell wonder-kid Sergio Agüero to Athletic Madrid for $34million (£17m) in 2006, yet the club's history is perhaps as glorious as any in Argentina—including a record seven Copa Libertadores titles. These include four in a row between 1972 and 1975, inspired by midfielder Ricardo Bochini, who played for 20 years with the club. They have also been home to the World Cup-winning trio of Daniel Bertoni, Jorge Burruchaga, and Oscar Ortiz.

Titles: Intercontinental Cup 1973, 1984; Copa Libertadores 1964, 1965, 1972, 1973, 1974, 1975, 1984; Argentine league 14 times

PEÑAROL (Uruguay)

Uruguay's most prestigious club provided the two scorers when Brazil were amazingly beaten in the 1950 World Cup finals, namely Alcides Ghigghia and Juan Schiaffino. At times in the 1960s, Peñarol could even outshine Pelé and Santos, including a 5-0 win in 1963, featuring a hat-trick by Pedro Spencer. He remains the all-time top scorer in the Copa Libertadores, leading the Montevideo club to three of their five triumphs. Peñarol have been crowned World Club champions three times.

Titles: Intercontinental Cup 1961, 1966, 1982;

Copa Libertadores 1960, 1961, 1966, 1982, 1987; Uruguayan league 37 times

RIVER PLATE (Argentina)

Along with Buenos Aires arch rivals Boca Juniors, River Plate remain one of Argentina's biggest, best-supported teams. Their formidable five-man forward line of the early 1940s was dubbed "La Máquina" (The Machine) but a sixth striker that decade was perhaps their greatest of all, Alfredo Di Stefano. Argentina's 1978 World Cup-winning captain Daniel Passarella spearheaded a club revival in the 1970s, before boyhood fan Hernan Crespo shot to fame at the Estadio Monumental in the 1990s. 1986 was a perfect year for River supporters—not only were Argentina crowned World Champions, but River captured the league, the Copa Libertadores, and the Club World Cup.
Titles: Intercontinental Cup 1986; Copa Libertadores 1986, 1996; Supercopa Sudamericana 1997; Copa Interamericana 1987; Argentine league 33 times

SANTOS (Brazil)

For much of the 1960s, Santos were the side the whole world wanted to see, thanks to their iconic No.10, Pelé. Besides clinching two world club titles—beating Benfica and AC Milan—and several state championships, the Brazilian entertainers toured the world almost non-stop to play money-making exhibition matches for huge crowds. Pelé's departure in 1972 inevitably signaled an end to the glory days, and they had to wait until 2002 for their next Brazilian league title. In recent years the club has produced such stars as Robinho, Elano, and Diego.
Titles: Intercontinental Cup 1962, 1963; Copa Libertadores 1962, 1963; Copa CONMEBOL 1998; Brazilian league champions 2, Brazilian Cup 1

SÃO PAULO (Brazil)

Brasilia is the country's capital, Rio's clubs have the most fervent support, and neighbors Santos boasted Pelé, but São Paulo can claim to be Brazil's most successful club. Leonidas da Silva in the 1940s, Gerson in the 1970s, Careca in the 1980s, and more recently Kaka have contributed to their collection of domestic and world titles. Their Copa Libertadores win in 2005 made them the first Brazilian club to claim a hat-trick of titles, and the first team to beat a side from the same country in the final, Atletico Paranaense.
Titles: Intercontinental Cup 1992, 1993, 2005; Copa Libertadores 1992, 1993, 2005; Copa CONMEBOL 1994; Brazilian league champions 5 times

VASCO DA GAMA (Brazil)

Vasco da Gama was founded in 1898 by Portuguese immigrants. The club takes its name from the Portuguese explorer of the 14th and 15th centuries, and gain much of their support from Rio's Portuguese community. World Cup-winning striker Romario started his career at Vasco in 1985 and retired in 2008 after his fourth term at the club, which included the goal he claimed was the 1,000th of his career. But his 316 goals for Vasco were less than half the tally of the club's leading goalscorer, Roberto Dinamite. He netted 698 in 1,110 games between 1971 and 1993. Vasco last won the Brazilian title in 2000.
Titles: Copa Libertadores 1998; Brazilian league champions 4 times

BELOW Pelé takes aim for Santos in 1973

GREAT CLUBS
REST OF THE WORLD

ABOVE Jaime Moreno of DC United looks for an opening against the New York Red Bulls

AL-AHLY (Egypt)

Little wonder the Cairo side were named in 2000 as the Confederation of African Football's club of the century. Egypt's so-called "People's Club" has won a record six African club championships, and a major haul of domestic titles. They even managed to remain unbeaten from 1974 to 1977. The "Red Devils," whose former players include Egypt's record scorer Hossam Hassan, have a ferocious rivalry with city rivals Zamalek. Foreign referees are often asked to handle their turbulent derby games.
Titles: African Champions League 1982, 1987, 2001, 2005, 2006, 2008; African Cup Winners' Cup 1984, 1985, 1986, 1993; African Super Cup 2005; Arab Champions Cup 1996; Arab Cup Winners' Cup 1994; Arab Super Cup 1997, 1998; Egyptian league 35 times, Egyptian cup 35

CLUB AMERICA (Mexico)

Club America have been Mexico's big spenders since a 1959 takeover by television giant Televisa. Until recent years at least, such power guaranteed success, including a record five CONCACAF Champions crowns (the same as arch rivals Cruz Azul) and ten league titles (Chivas have won 11 championships). Big-name foreign imports have included Argentina's Oscar Ruggeri, Chilean Ivan Zamorano, and Romania's Ilie Dumitrescu. But they have also developed home-grown talent such as Mexican playmaker Cuauhtemoc Blanco. Club America play at the 114,465-capacity Azteca in Mexico City, the only stadium to have hosted two World Cup finals.
Titles: CONCACAF Champions Cup 1978, 1987, 1991, 1993, 2006; CONCACAF Cup Winners' Cup 2001; Copa Interamericana 1978, 1991; Mexican league 10 times, Mexican cup 5

DC UNITED (United States)

Captain John Harkes, returning home from the English Premier League, and coach Bruce Arena led the Washington DC-based club to the first two MLS titles in 1996 and 1997. They also became the first US club to win the CONCACAF Champions' Cup in 1998. But trophies have proved harder to come by since Arena left to become national coach in 1998, despite high-profile signings such as iconic Hristo Stoichkov and Freddy Adu—who made his debut aged 14.
Titles: CONCACAF Champions Cup 1998; Copa Interamericana 1998; US MLS Cup 4 times; US Open Cup 1

ETOILE SAHEL (Tunisia)

Tunisia may have underachieved internationally, with only one African Cup of Nations triumph. But their oldest club has proved the pride of a nation, with impressive performances in all CAF competitions. Dynamic young striker Armine Chermiti helped them achieve surprise Champions League glory in 2007. Victory over holders Al-Ahly, made them the first club to have won each of the African Federation's club trophies.
Titles: African Champions League 2007; CAF Cup 2006; African Cup Winners' Cup 1997, 2003; African Super Cup 1998, 2008; Tunisian league 8 times; President's Cup 7; League Cup 1

LOS ANGELES GALAXY (United States)

LA Galaxy pulled off the most high-profile signing in MLS history when England superstar David Beckham joined from Real Madrid in 2007. Another great, Holland's Ruud Gullit, was then appointed Galaxy coach but lasted less than a year in charge. Beckham's arrival helped the club sell 700 times as many replica shirts as before, and

inspire hope among directors and fans that they might win the CONCACAF Champions League Cup for a second time. Long-serving Cobi Jones was among the scorers when they won in 2000.
Titles: CONCACAF Champions Cup 2000; US MLS Cup 2; US Open Cup 2

KAIZER CHIEFS (South Africa)

Kaizer Chiefs, one of South Africa's first professional clubs, take their name from the former international midfielder, Kaizer Motaung. He co-founded the club in 1970 after returning from a spell in the US. He has since served them as a player, in three separate stints as coach, and now as club president. The Chiefs passionately contest the Soweto derby with Orlando Pirates, another of Motaung's old teams. Their home at Johannesburg's FNB Stadium was rebuilt as Soccer City to host the 2010 World Cup final.
Titles: African Cup Winners' Cup 2001; South African league 11 (including former National Soccer League and National Premier Soccer League titles)

POHANG STEELERS (South Korea)

Pohang Steelers dominated in the 1970s and 1980s, then suffered a 15-year barren spell in the K-League until their 2007 title triumph. In 1997, they became the third South Korean team to win the Asian Champions League by beating compatriots and defending champions Seongham Ilhwa Chunma. They retained the trophy the following year against China's Dalian Wanda. They beat Saudi side Al-Ittihad in 2009 to claim a record third title. Center back Hong-Myung Bo, his country's most-capped player, is probably the famous of Steelers' stars.
Titles: Asian Champions League 1997, 1998, 2009; South Korean league 4 times; South Korean cup 2

UNAM PUMAS (Mexico)

UNAM Pumas, the club affiliated to Latin America's largest university, has long put an emphasis on youth and produced Mexican legends such as Luis Garcia, Jorge Campos, and Hugo Sanchez. Inspirational striker Sanchez scored 96 goals for Pumas from 1976 to 1981, then returned as coach 19 years later, guiding the club to four trophies in 2004. Goalkeeper Campos loved to roam upfield. He also sometimes switched to play in attack and scored 35 goals in 199 games. Pumas' home in Mexico City was the main venue for the 1968 Olympics Games.
Titles: CONCACAF Champions Cup 1980, 1982, 1989; Copa Interamericana 1981; Mexican league 6 times, Mexican cup 1

URAWA RED DIAMONDS (Japan)

Urawa Red Diamonds won four league titles and four Emperor's Cups before the Japanese game turned professional in 1993. They made a bad start in the J.League, finishing bottom in the first two seasons. The team nicknamed "The Nearly Men" lived up to their image by just missing out on the 2004 and 2005 titles. But they finally sparkled, to become J.League champions in 2006 and win the Asian Champions League in 2007. Star players have included Japanese midfielder Shinji Ono and Brazilian striker Edmundo.
Titles: Asian Champions League 2007; Japanese league 5 times; Emperor's Cup 6; J.League Cup 1

BELOW Urawa Reds Diamonds take the glory after their Asian Champions League triumph in 2007

GREAT MANAGERS

Great managers come in many forms. Some were
visionary tacticians. Others were motivators, drawing
the very best from their players. Some were shrewd
talent spotters, others great strategists. Some were
showmen, others quiet men who preferred the
background. But all were history makers, from
Arsenal's Herbert Chapman in the 1930s to Spain's
World Cup boss Vicente Del Bosque.

GREAT MANAGERS

ABOVE Sir Matt Busby (right) admires George Best's European footballer prize

PAGE 176 Sir Alex Ferguson makes a winning point in training

PAGE 177 Vicente del Bosque celebrates with his players after their World Cup win in the 2010 tournament

CARLO ANCELOTTI (born 10 June 1959)
Greatest successes: European Champions League 2003, 2007 (AC Milan)
Ancelotti has won the European Champions Cup twice each as player and coach. He was midfield anchor for Milan's 1989 and 1990 triumphs, then steered them to victory in 2003 and 2007—and suffered defeat on penalty kicks in the 2005 final after they led Liverpool 3-0. He took charge at Milan in 2001 after spells at Reggiana, Parma and Juventus. He steered them to the Italian title in 2004 but the Champions League often seemed their top priority. Ancelotti became expert at

dealing with Milan's demanding owner, Silvio Berlusconi. He used those skills to good effect after Roman Abramovich brought him to Chelsea in 2009. Ancelotti introduced a more attacking style and Chelsea won the 2010 Premiership and FA Cup double in his first season.

VICENTE DEL BOSQUE (Born 23 December 1950)
Greatest successes: World Cup 2010 (Spain); European Champions League 2000, 2002 (Real Madrid)
Del Bosque stepped from the shadows to revive Real Madrid, then found even greater glory guiding Spain's World Cup winners in 2010. His calmness was a key factor in their recovery after a shock opening defeat by Switzerland. The former Spain midfielder succeeded John Toshack at Madrid in November 1999, stabilized the squad and steered them to a Champions League victory over Valencia. Two years later, they beat Bayer Leverkusen to win the trophy again. They also added Spanish titles in 2001 and 2003. But Del Bosque was at odds with president Florentino Perez over transfers—and he was sacked the day after the 2003 Spanish league success. He turned down an offer to coach Mexico in 2006 before succeeding Luis Aragones as Spain coach in July 2008.

Sir MATT BUSBY (born 26 May 1909, died 20 January 1994)
Greatest success: European Cup 1968 (Manchester United)
Busby managed Manchester United between 1945 and 1969 and as a caretaker for part of the 1970–71 season. He created the "Busby Babes" who won the league in 1956 and 1957. After the 1958 Munich air crash—in which 23 people died,

including eight players—he built another great side from the survivors and new stars such as George Best. Busby's crowning glory was the 4-1 defeat of Benfica in the European Cup final at Wembley in 1968. It was the first time an English team had won the trophy.

FABIO CAPELLO (born 18 June 1946)
Greatest success: 1994 European Cup (AC Milan)
The Italian was appointed England's coach in December 2007. He had previously won the league title with every club he had managed: AC Milan (four times), Real Madrid (twice), Roma, and Juventus. He also coached Milan to their 4-0 thrashing of Johan Cruyff's Barcelona in the 1994 Champions League final.

BRIAN CLOUGH (born 21 March 1935, died 20 September 2004)
Greatest successes: 1979 and 1980 European Cups (Nottingham Forest)
Clough was the first manager since Herbert Chapman to win the English championship with two different clubs (Derby County and Nottingham Forest). He was an iconic if idiosyncratic manager who could draw the best out of problematic players. His outspoken manner did not always endear himself to players—he lasted only 44 days at Leeds United in 1974.

HERBERT CHAPMAN (born 19 January 1878, died 6 January 1934)
Greatest successes: 1924, 1925, 1931, and 1933 English league titles (Huddersfield Town and Arsenal)
Chapman is associated indelibly with Arsenal in the 1930s, but he made his name as a manager of Huddersfield Town in the 1920s. He laid out a five-year plan for success for Arsenal, which came to fruition exactly on schedule when his team won the 1930 FA Cup at the expense of his former club, Huddersfield. The victory laid the foundations for a decade in which Arsenal dominated English football.

VICENTE FEOLA (born 1 November 1909, died 6 November 1975)
Greatest success: 1958 World Cup (Brazil)
Feola famously guided Brazil to their first World Cup triumph in Sweden, although he took some persuading from senior players to pick both Garrincha and Pelé in the middle of the tournament when they appeared to be floundering. He missed Brazil's successful defense of the World Cup in 1962 because of illness. He returned for the luckless 1966 finals in England, when his side went out at the group stage. Feola finished with an outstanding career record, only losing six matches of the 74 his team played.

SIR ALEX FERGUSON (born 31 December 1941)
Greatest successes: 1999 and 2008 European Cups (Manchester United)
Ferguson has become English football's most successful manager ever since taking over at Manchester United in 1986. His teams have won 11 of the 18 championships in the Premier League era, the last in 2009. Ferguson was lured south from Aberdeen, which he had famously guided to victory over Real Madrid in the 1983 European Cup Winners' Cup final. His success began with an FA Cup win in 1990, and included an incredible treble of winning the Champions League, Premier League, and FA Cup in 1999. He came close to a repeat in 2008, winning the Premier League and the Champions League in the 50th anniversary year of the Munich air crash.

JOSEF "SEPP" HERBERGER
(born 28 March 1897, died 20 April 1977)
Greatest success: 1954 World Cup (West Germany)
Herberger became manager of Germany in 1938 and used all his sports and political influence to

ABOVE Fabio Capello, star midfielder turned star manager

BELOW Sepp Herberger plots the "Miracle of Bern"

GREAT MANAGERS

try to keep his players away from the battlefronts during World War II. He returned as national manager after the war and won West Germany's first World Cup in 1954. The final was aptly labeled the "Miracle of Berne" after his team beat hot favorites Hungary 3-2.

HELENIO HERRERA (born 17 April 1910, died 9 November 1997)
Greatest successes: 1964 World Club and European Cups (Internazionale)
Herrera, known widely in his heyday simply as "HH," managed a number of top clubs and national teams (including Italy and Spain), winning 16 major trophies. Born in Morocco but brought up in Argentina, he played in France before concentrating on coaching in France, Spain, and Italy. Herrera pioneered the use of psychological motivational ploys and, more controversially,

artificial substances.

GUUS HIDDINK (born 8 November 1946)
Greatest success: 1988 European Cup (PSV Eindhoven)
Hiddink sprang to prominence as PSV coach in the late 1980s. He later coached Valencia and Real Madrid in Spain before leading South Korea to a fourth place finish in the 2002 World Cup. He had previously managed the Dutch national team at Euro '96. In a second spell at PSV, he steered them to their first Champions League semi-final appearance in 2005. He also led Australia to the finals of the 2006 World Cup for the first time in 32 years. Hiddink then revitalized the Russian national team, guiding them to the semi-finals of Euro 2008. He is currently coach of Turkey.

VALERI LOBANOVSKI (born 6 January 1939, died 13 May 2002)
Greatest successes: 1975 and 1986 European Cup Winners' Cups (Dynamo Kiev)
Lobanovski was a hero in Ukraine before the collapse of the Soviet Union. He was the Dynamo Kiev manager for 15 years, twice winning the Cup Winners' Cup and also beating Bayern Munich to take the 1975 European Supercup. Lobanovski spent three spells managing the Soviet Union and also managed Ukraine.

CÉSAR LUIS MENOTTI (born 5 November 1938)
Greatest success: 1978 World Cup (Argentina)
In 1978, the left-leaning César Luis Menotti made himself immune from action by the ruling military junta because he was busy leading Argentina to their first-ever World Cup success. Menotti believed in positive, attacking football, which set

BELOW Guus Hiddink trains his team in preparation for the 2008 UEFA European Championship

him at odds with other top Argentine coaches of the era such as Juan Carlos Lorenzo and Osvaldo Zubeldía. Menotti quit after Argentina's second round group exit at the 1982 finals in Spain, after defeat at the hands of Brazil and Italy.

JOSE MOURINHO (born 26 January 1963)
Greatest successes: European Champions League 2004 (Porto), 2010 (Internazionale)
Mourinho, the self-styled "Special One," boasts the achievements to support his nickname. He first made an impression as coach of unfashionable Portuguese club Uniao Leiria. He took over at Porto in 2002, winning the Portuguese league title and the UEFA Cup in his first season. The following season Porto won the European Champions League and the domestic championship. Mourinho then steered Chelsea to their first English title for 50 years and added another before falling out with owner Roman Abramovich. He guided Internazionale to the Italian crown in 2009 and the treble of European Champions League, Serie A, and Coppa Italia in 2010. Inter's first Champions Cup success since 1965 was achieved against Bayern Munich in the home stadium of Real Madrid—who he joined immediately after the final.

BOB PAISLEY (born 23 January 1919, died 14 February 1996)
Greatest successes: 1977, 1978, and 1981 European Cups (Liverpool)
Paisley stepped up, virtually unknown outside Anfield, from the role of assistant when Bill Shankly retired unexpectedly in 1974. During his nine years in charge, Paisley guided Liverpool to six league titles. He remains the only man to have managed one club to three European Cup successes. He won 19 major titles in all.

VITTORIO POZZO (born 12 March 1886, died 21 December 1968)
Greatest successes: 1934 and 1938 World Cups, 1936 Olympic Games (Italy)
Pozzo, who was also a journalist, learned to love football during a period of study in England. In 1934 he had no doubts about using former Argentina internationals, such as Luis Monti and Raimundo Orsi, to strengthen his first World Cup-winning side. Ruthlessly, he then scrapped almost the entire team to build a new side for the 1938 competition. In between these triumphs, Pozzo guided Italy to gold medal success at the 1936 Olympic Games. Pozzo retired in 1949 after the Superga air disaster wiped out the entire playing staff of Torino, around whom he was planning to build a team for the 1950 World Cup.

SIR ALF RAMSEY (born 22 January 1920, died 28 April 1999)
Greatest success: 1966 World Cup (England)
Ramsey will always hold a special place in English football history as the only manager to have brought the country success in a major competition. A year after his achievement, he was knighted. However, Ramsey was forced out in early 1974 because of England's unexpected failure to qualify for the World Cup finals in West Germany.

ABOVE Vittorio Pozzo holds aloft the World Cup trophy after his team's victory in the 1938 tournament

BELOW Sir Alf Ramsey in training in 1974

Jose Mourinho (far right) celebrates with his Inter Milan team after their 2-0 win over Bayern Munich in the 2010 Champions League final

GREAT MANAGERS

SIR BOBBY ROBSON (born 18 February 1933, died 31 July 2009)
Greatest successes: 1978 FA Cup, 1981 UEFA Cup (Ipswich Town)
Robson was a managerial legend at Ipswich Town, where he remained for 13 years before his England call-up. At club level, Robson's side twice finished as runner-up in the league, but made amends by capturing the FA Cup in 1978 and lifting the UEFA Cup in 1981. Robson moved abroad to win league championships in both Holland and Portugal. He later took England to the brink of the 1990 World Cup final—they fell only in a penalty shoot-out to West Germany—before returning to club management.

ARRIGO SACCHI (born 1 April 1946)
Greatest successes: 1989 and 1990 European Cups (AC Milan)
Sacchi never played football professionally but more than made up for that as a coach. "You don't need to have been a horse to become a successful jockey" was arguably one of his best quotes. He had been plucked from Serie B obscurity by Silvio Berlusconi, the new AC Milan owner, in the mid 1980s, and swiftly introduced a new, positive, and—most importantly—winning approach to the Italian game. Milan's squad was bursting with talent, including the trio of Dutchmen Ruud Gullit, Marco Van Basten, and Frank Rijkaard. His Milan successes led to an appointment as coach of Italy, who finished as runners-up to Brazil in the 1994 World Cup.

HELMUT SCHÖN (born 15 September 1915, died 23 February 1996)
Greatest success: 1974 World Cup (West Germany)
Under Schön's 14-year leadership, West Germany won the World Cup on home territory in 1974, after finishing third at Mexico in 1970 and runner-up to England in 1966. West Germany hosted the World Cup finals as worthy winners of the 1972 European Championship under Schön. He is the only manager to have won both the World Cup and European Championship and hold the titles simultaneously.

RIGHT Bill Shankly laid the foundations for the Liverpool revival

BILL SHANKLY (born 2 September 1913, died 29 September 1981)
Greatest successes: 1966 and 1973 English league titles, 1973 UEFA Cup (Liverpool)
Shankly is remembered by Liverpool fans as their greatest ever manager, his legend embellished by a string of witty one-liners such as: "some people believe football is a matter of life and death. I can assure you it is much, much more important than that." Liverpool had been a club stuck in the second division doldrums when Shankly took over in 1959, but he soon transformed it on and off the field, and developed a unique team spirit and identity that lives on to this day. He secured Liverpool's inaugural European trophy in 1973, courtesy of a UEFA Cup final victory over Borussia Mönchengladbach.

JOCK STEIN (born 5 October 1922, died 10 September 1985)
Greatest success: 1967 European Cup (Celtic)
Jock Stein was one of the most successful Scottish managers ever. Between 1965 and 1978, his Celtic side lifted the European Cup, ten Scottish League titles, eight Scottish Cups, and six Scottish League Cups. Stein's Celtic became the first British club to win the European Cup when his "Lisbon Lions" defeated Internazionale in 1967 in Portugal. He took over as Scotland's manager in 1978, where he remained until he died of a heart attack just after his Scottish side had equalized against Wales and earned a place in the 1986 World Cup finals.

GIOVANNI TRAPATTONI (born 17 March 1939)
Greatest success: 1985 European Cup (Juventus)
Giovanni Trapattoni is Italy's most successful club manager, winning seven Serie A titles and the European Cup. He and Germany's Udo Lattek are the only managers to have won all three major European club titles. He had a glittering career as an AC Milan defender, where he twice won the European Cup. Trapattoni has a wealth of experience, having coached both Milan clubs, Fiorentina, Juventus, Bayern Munich (twice), Benfica, Stuttgart, and Red Bull Salzburg, with an impressive record of ten domestic titles in four countries. He was also in charge of the Azzurri from 2000 to 2004, but his side struggled in both the 2002 World Cup finals and 2004 European Championship. In May 2008, he became coach of the Republic of Ireland.

ARSÈNE WENGER (born 22 October 1949)
Greatest successes: 1998 and 2002 English league and FA Cup doubles (Arsenal)
Arsène Wenger made a major contribution in transforming the English game after being brought in by Arsenal in 1996. He was comparatively unknown when he first arrived, despite being both successful and respected in France and Japan. Since then, Wenger has guided Arsenal to three league titles and four FA Cup triumphs, including league and cup doubles in 1998 and 2002. Remarkably, in 2003–04, his side completed an entire 38-match Premier League season unbeaten. He is the club's most successful and longest-serving manager.

MARIO ZAGALLO (born 9 August 1931)
Greatest success: 1970 World Cup (Brazil)
Mario Zagallo is a Brazilian icon, having enjoyed a magnificent career, both as a player and a coach. He played as an industrious left-winger in the World Cup-winning sides in 1958 and 1962, then graduated to manage the side in 1970, winning the 1970 finals in Mexico. With this victory, he became the first person to win the World Cup as both a player and a coach. His career with Brazil has continued in various roles, including the post of technical director at the 2006 World Cup finals. His Brazilian team won the World Cup in 1994 but finished as runner-up to France in the 1998 World Cup finals.

ABOVE Giovanni Trapattoni makes a point during a Republic of Ireland match

BELOW Arsène Wenger guided Arsenal to two domestic doubles

1930s   1940s   1960s

ABOVE Herbert Chapman, Arsenal's first great manager

BELOW Jimmy Hogan staging a coaching lesson for troops

ABOVE Matt Busby with his 1968 Manchester United team

RIGHT England boss Sir Alf Ramsey (right) with Bobby Charlton

BELOW Sepp Herberger (left) talks tactics with German journalist Friedebert Becker

1970s

1990s

2000s

ABOVE Nottingham Forest's Brian Clough in trademark green jumper

ABOVE Sir Bobby Robson points the way for Newcastle

ABOVE Giovanni Trapattoni gets a message to his players

ABOVE Mario Zagallo, a World Cup winner as player and manager

ABOVE Arsène Wenger took Arsenal to the double in his first full season

LEFT Sir Alex Ferguson guided Manchester United to new glory

GREAT PLAYERS

Great players are the lifeblood of football. Early heroes
have passed into legend, captured only on old
newsreels. Modern greats are admired across the
planet. The 1970 World Cup marked a decisive step in
the fame game as the first finals broadcast worldwide
in color—adding to the luster of successive stars from
Pelé through to Lionel Messi.

GREAT PLAYERS
EUROPEAN PLAYERS

PAGE 188 Ryan Giggs in action for Manchester United in a 2010 Premier League match against Newcastle

PAGE 189 Thierry Henry playing for Arsenal against PSV Eindhoven

MARCO VAN BASTEN (born 31 October 1964)

Holland: 58 games, 24 goals

Marco Van Basten scored one of the finest goals in international history when he volleyed home Holland's second in their victory over the Soviet Union in the 1988 European Championship final. The goal sealed Van Basten's reputation as one of the finest center forwards to grace European football, not only with Holland but also with top club sides Ajax Amsterdam and AC Milan. Injury forced his premature retirement.

FRANZ BECKENBAUER (born 11 September 1945)

West Germany: 103 games, 14 goals

Franz Beckenbauer is one of the few defenders guaranteed a place in any football hall of fame. Initially a playmaker, "Der Kaiser" was converted into a creative sweeper by Yugoslav coach Tschi Cajkovski at Bayern Munich in the 1960s. He won every honor at domestic level and lifted the World Cup as the West German captain in 1974 and again as national coach in 1990. In recent years he has served as president of Bayern and as a member of the FIFA executive. He also chaired the organizing committee for the 2006 World Cup in Germany.

DAVID BECKHAM (born 2 May 1975)

England: 115 games, 17 goals

A boyhood Manchester United fan, David Beckham went on to win a historic treble with the club in 1999. He was subsequently sold to Real Madrid in 2003, winning the Spanish league in the last of his four seasons with them, then joined LA Galaxy. He was loaned to AC Milan during the Major League Soccer close season in 2009 and 2010. Beckham

played in three World Cup finals for England, but missed out on the 2010 tournament because of an Achilles tendon injury.

GEORGE BEST (born 22 May 1946, died 25 November 2005)

Northern Ireland: 37 games, 9 goals

Best was arguably the greatest player never to have made an appearance in the World Cup finals. A magical talent, one of the most exciting to grace English football, he made his Manchester United debut as a winger aged 17 in 1963 and went on to win the European Cup in 1968 and two league titles, before being driven out of the British game by the pressures of his own fame. His greatest exploit was in United's 5-1 thrashing of Benfica in Lisbon in a European Cup quarter-final in 1966. He was voted European Footballer of the Year in 1968.

LIAM BRADY (born 13 February 1956)

Republic of Ireland: 72 games, 9 goals

RIGHT George Best, both European Champion and European Footballer of the Year in 1968

Liam Brady was the cultured midfield general of the Arsenal side which reached the FA Cup final three times in a row between 1978 and 1980, gaining a winner's medal in 1979. He moved to Juventus the following year and helped them win Serie A titles in 1981 and 1982. He joined Sampdoria after Michel Platini's arrival at Juventus and later played for Internazionale and Ascoli. He returned to England with West Ham United before retiring and later rejoining Arsenal where he is currently director of the youth academy. Brady is also part-time assistant to Republic of Ireland coach Giovanni Trapattoni, his former boss at Juventus.

GIANLUIGI BUFFON

(born 28 January 1978)

Italy: 102 games

"Gigi" Buffon has been one of the world's top goalkeepers for more than a decade. He made his first international appearance at the age of 19 and has since passed a century of caps. He kept five clean sheets and conceded just two goals in the finals when Italy won the World Cup in 2006. He began his club career with Parma in 1995, then joined Juventus six years later. The fee of $50 million (£25 m) was a world record for a keeper. He helped Parma win the UEFA Cup and the Coppa Italia in 1999 and gained four league title medals with Juventus (though two were later erased from the records). He stayed with them when they were relegated in 2006 after a bribe scandal, despite lucrative offers from several rivals.

IKER CASILLAS (born 20 May 1981)

Spain: 116 games

Casillas became Real Madrid's goalkeeper as a teenager. He was the youngest-ever keeper to play in a Champions League final when he helped them beat Valencia in 2000 four days after his 19th birthday. He was a substitute in Real's victory over Bayer Leverkusen two years later when his saves foiled the Germans' late rally. He has made more than 500 appearances for the club and is now their skipper. He also captained Spain to victory

ABOVE Gianluigi Buffon in action for Italy in a 2001 friendly match against Argentina

at Euro 2008 and the 2010 World Cup finals. He was outstanding at the 2008 finals and recovered from a mistake in the opening game to star again in South Africa. He has won 116 caps and is on course to beat Andoni Zubizarreta's national record of 126.

SIR BOBBY CHARLTON (born 11 October 1937)

England: 106 games, 49 goals

Bobby Charlton had just established himself in the Manchester United side when the squad was tragically torn apart by the 1958 Munich air crash—eight players died in the disaster. Charlton survived and helped lead the reconstruction of the devastated United side. Ten years later, he captained them to victory in the European Cup. He scored two goals in the 4-1 victory over Benfica in the final at Wembley. Two years earlier, Charlton's unerring shooting had helped fire England to their sole success as World Cup winners. He was briefly manager of Preston before returning to his beloved Manchester United as a director. He was knighted in 1994.

Kevin Kuranyi of Germany and Iker Casillas of Spain challenge for the ball during the 2008 European Championship final

BELOW Johan Cruyff, a club champion of Europe as both player and coach

JOHAN CRUYFF (born 25 April 1947)

Holland: 48 games, 33 goals

Johan Cruyff, son of a cleaner at the Ajax Amsterdam offices, grew up to be the epitome of Holland's "Total Football" revolution, as well as being voted European Footballer of the Year three times in the 1970s. Ajax's unique style of play brought the club—and Cruyff—three successive victories in the European Cup. Cruyff, despite being the club's captain, was sold to Barcelona for the then world record fee of $1.85 million (£922,000) prior to the 1974 World Cup finals, where hosts West Germany edged past the Dutch 2-1 in the final. Cruyff controversially refused to play in the 1978 World Cup finals in Argentina, because of the kidnap threats made to him and his family. Holland reached the final, but critics believe that with his presence they could have returned with the trophy. When he returned to Ajax as technical director, the side went on to win the 1987 European Cup Winners' Cup. He later managed Barcelona, building their "Dream Team" which he guided to victory in the 1992 European Champions Cup.

KENNY DALGLISH (born 4 March 1951)

Scotland: 102 games, 30 goals

Kenny Dalglish achieved a remarkable feat by winning league titles as both a player and a manager in England with Liverpool and as a player in Scotland with Celtic. A nimble, quick-thinking forward, Dalglish moved from Glasgow to Liverpool in 1977 as replacement for the legendary Kevin Keegan. He duly proved that he could fill the boots of the Kop hero—he was the club's leading scorer in his first season. After a glittering playing career for Liverpool, he

successfully made the transition to managing the club in 1985, and became the only player-manager in modern times to steer his club to a domestic double of both league and FA Cup. Dalglish also equaled Denis Law's scoring record for Scotland—and stands alone with the record for most appearances.

DIXIE DEAN (born 22 January 1907, died 1 March 1980)

England: 16 games, 18 goals

Dixie Dean remains the most prolific striker in English football history after rattling home 60 goals in just 39 matches for Everton in the 1927–28 season. His record is virtually untouchable, but the center forward was merely taking advantage of a recent change to the offside law. Dean's incredible career total of 349 goals in 399 games helped Everton collect two league titles and one FA Cup. He only played 16 times for England, but scored 18 goals in those games.

EUSÉBIO (born 25 January 1942)

Portugal: 64 games, 41 goals

Eusébio da Silva Ferreira, a Mozambican-born Portuguese striker, was nicknamed the "Black Panther" for his valuable goals. He inspired Benfica to a 5-3 victory over Real Madrid in the European Cup in 1962, although his team could only finish as the runner-up in the same competition in 1963, 1965, and 1968. During the 15 years Eusébio spent at Benfica, he won the Portuguese league title ten times. In the 1966 World Cup finals in England, he guided Portugal to third place and won the Golden Boot as top scorer in the competition with nine goals. His finest performance was in the memorable quarter-final against North Korea. The Koreans raced to a 3-0 lead before Eusébio scored four goals to give his country a 5-3 victory.

GIACINTO FACCHETTI (born 18 July 1942, died 4 September 2006)
Italy: 94 games, 3 goals

Facchetti was the first of Europe's great attacking full backs. The Internazionale defender was a menace in open play and at dead ball moves. He netted 59 league goals in 476 league appearances as Inter won four championships between 1962 and 1971. He helped them win the European Cup in 1964 and netted the semi-final clincher against Liverpool on their way to retaining the trophy a year later. He gained 94 caps for Italy. He starred in their 1968 European Championship-winning side and played in the 1970 World Cup final against Brazil. He was Inter's president from 19 January 2004, until his premature death two years later. The club then "retired" his No3 shirt as a mark of respect for his achievements.

JUST FONTAINE (born 18 August 1933)
France: 21 games, 30 goals

Just Fontaine was a fast, brave center forward who wrote his name into World Cup history by scoring 13 goals for third-placed France in the 1958 finals—he scored in all six games. Fontaine, born in Morocco, was brought to France to play for Nice, with whom he won the French League title in 1956. He was then sold to the great Reims side that dominated French football at the time. In the 1957–58 season, his goals helped secure the double of the French league and cup for Reims. Yet Fontaine only got his chance in the 1958 World Cup finals because Reims team-mate Rene Bliard was ruled out with an ankle injury. Fontaine's career was ended prematurely in 1961, because of two serious leg fractures. He won the domestic league four times and the French Cup twice.

FRANCISCO GENTO (born 21 October 1933)
Spain: 43 games, 5 goals

"Paco" Gento set a record in 1966 when, as captain of Real Madrid, he collected a sixth European Cup winner's medal. Gento, from Santander in northern Spain, was nicknamed "El Supersonico" for his electric pace on the left wing. His distracting effect created valuable extra space to assist the goalscoring exploits of team-mates such as Alfredo Di Stefano and Ferenc Puskás. Gento was a key figure in Real Madrid's triumphs of the 1950s and 1960s, scoring 126 goals in 428 games over 18 years. He won the domestic league title 12 times, represented Spain in the 1962 and 1966 World Cup finals, and played a key role in the side that dominated the first five European Cup finals with successive victories in the late 1950s.

BELOW Just Fontaine in triumph after scoring four goals against West Germany in the 1958 World Cup

EUROPEAN PLAYERS

RYAN GIGGS (born 29 November 1973)
Wales: 64 games, 12 goals
Wales winger Giggs is—like his famous Manchester United predecessor George Best—one of the finest players never to have appeared at the World Cup finals. But he has been hugely influential for United. He began as a goalscoring left winger. His winner against Arsenal in the 1999 semi-final replay was one of the finest in modern FA Cup history. He later dropped back to become a cunning midfielder. He is the only player to have scored in every Premier League season since its inception in 1992. He has appeared in all United's 11 Premiership title-winning seasons. He also starred in their 1999 and 2008 European Champions League wins. Giggs has helped United win the FA Cup four times and been a League Cup winner on three occasions.

BELOW Ruud Gullit (left) blasts the ball past Thomas Berthold during the 1990 World Cup

RUUD GULLIT (born 1 September 1962)
Holland: 66 games, 17 goals
Ruud Gullit was hailed as Europe's finest player in the late 1980s, when he moved from Dutch football to help inspire a revival at AC Milan. Gullit, World Player of the Year in 1987 and 1989, was a favorite of Milan owner Silvio Berlusconi, winning two European Cups and three Italian league titles. He captained Holland in the 1988 European Championship, heading home the opening goal in the 2-0 victory over Russia in the final. He moved to Chelsea as a player and later became their coach—he was the first non-British manager to win the FA Cup. He subsequently had brief spells as manager of Newcastle United, Feyenoord in Holland, and LA Galaxy.

GHEORGHE HAGI (born 5 February 1965)
Romania: 125 games, 35 goals
Gheorghe Hagi was nicknamed the "Maradona of the Carpathians" during the late 1980s because of his cultured left foot and silky skills. His huge self-confidence helped him to push forward from midfield to score goals, but his main strength lay in his skill and vision as a playmaker. Such outstanding talent earned special permission, in a restrictive political era, to go abroad to ply his trade. He played for Real Madrid, moved on to Brescia in Italy, and then to Barcelona before ending his career at Turkish side Galatasaray. Hagi was the fulcrum of the Romanian side that reached the quarter-finals of the 1994 World Cup.

THIERRY HENRY (born 17 August 1977)
France: 123 games, 51 goals
Thierry Henry set a scoring record for Arsenal

over eight seasons, proving to be a bargain signing even at $21 million (£10.5 m) when he was bought from Juventus in 1999. He won championship medals in 2002 and 2004. He also won World Cup and European Championship medals with France. He joined Barcelona in 2007 and helped them win the treble—European Champions League, Spanish championship and cup—in 2009. He earned another Spanish title medal in 2010, before joining New York Red Bulls in Major League Soccer.

SIR GEOFF HURST (born 8 December 1941)

England: 49 games, 24 goals

Sir Geoff Hurst remains the only player to have scored a hat-trick in a World Cup final, an achievement which ultimately earned him a belated knighthood. Hurst only came into the England side because Jimmy Greaves was injured. As well as his match-winning performance in the final, Hurst scored what proved to be the decisive goal in the quarter-final against Argentina.

ANDRES INIESTA (born 11 May 1984)

Spain: 54 games, 9 goals

Iniesta clinched his place in football history by scoring Spain's extra time winner against Holland in the 2010 World Cup final. The Barcelona midfielder was also one of the heroes of his country's Euro 2008 victory. His midfield partnership with Xavi has been crucial to so many successes, for club and country. He made his club debut in October 2002 and has been a regular ever since. He has played an important role in Barcelona winning the European Champions League in 2006 and 2009—besides four league titles and the domestic King's Cup in 2009. After the 2009 final, Manchester United's Wayne Rooney called him "the best player in the world."

MIROSLAV KLOSE (born 9 June 1978)

Germany: 105 games, 58 goals

Klose was born in Poland, but has become one of Germany's most prolific strikers. His father was

ABOVE Thierry Henry, a record marksman with both Arsenal and France

LEFT Geoff Hurst (far right) heads home his first goal in the 1966 World Cup final

Argentina's (left to right) Nicolas Burdisso, goalkeeper Sergio Romero and Gabriel Heinze can only watch as Germany's Miroslav Klose (far right) heads towards goal during a 2010 World Cup quarter-final match

GREAT PLAYERS
EUROPEAN PLAYERS

German and Miroslav believed that his football future lay there. He has made a major impact in three World Cup finals tournaments, starting in 2002. Klose has netted 14 World Cup goals, equal with the great Gerd Muller. He was top scorer in the 2006 finals with five. He is known for his power in the air and his lethal right foot. Klose has won 105 caps for Germany and scored 58 goals. He celebrated his 100th appearance with two in the 4-0 win over Argentina in the 2010 World Cup quarter-finals. Klose made his name with Kaiserslautern. He moved on to Werder Bremen, then Bayern Munich.

RAYMOND KOPA (born 13 October 1931)
France: 45 games, 18 goals
Raymond Kopa was born into a Polish mining family in northern France. His talent was first spotted by Angers, who sold him on to Reims in 1950. He was sold to Real Madrid after the Spanish club defeated Reims in the European Cup final in 1956. At Real Madrid he won the European Cup three times and was crowned 1958 European Footballer of the Year. Kopa won four French and two Spanish league titles.

HANS KRANKL (born 14 February 1953)
Austria: 69 games, 34 goals
Hans Krankl was one of the great Austrian center forwards. In 1978 he scored 41 goals for Rapid Vienna, winning the Golden Boot as Europe's leading league scorer. He starred for Austria at the World Cup finals in Argentina, where he netted the winning goal against West Germany—Austria's first victory over their neighbors for 37 years. He went on to play for Barcelona, where he won the 1979 European Cup Winners' Cup.

MICHAEL LAUDRUP (born 15 June 1964)
Denmark: 104 games, 37 goals
Michael Laudrup stood out in Denmark's outstanding team that reached the semi-finals of the 1984 European Championship and the second round at the 1986 World Cup finals. He achieved club success with Juventus before moving to Lazio, and he was part of Johan Cruyff's "Dream Team" at Barcelona where he won four league titles. He also played for Real Madrid and Ajax.

DENIS LAW (born 24 February 1940)
Scotland: 55 games, 30 goals
Denis Law, whatever the competing talents of Bobby Charlton and George Best, was the king of Old Trafford in the 1960s. His ebullient personality, and his ability to create chances and goals out of nothing, earned him the adulation of Manchester United fans. Law started at Huddersfield Town, and had brief spells at Manchester City and Torino before being brought to United in 1962.

RIGHT Denis Law takes the high road for Manchester United at Old Trafford

He repaid the club's financial investment with 171 goals in 309 league games. He won the European Footballer of the Year prize in 1964.

GARY LINEKER (born 30 November 1960)
England: 80 games, 48 goals

Gary Lineker made his name with hometown Leicester City, but his career took off after his transfer to Everton in 1985. Lineker moved on to Barcelona, winning the European Cup Winners' Cup, and in the 1986 World Cup finals he won the Golden Boot as the leading scorer with six goals. The prolific striker returned to England for a successful spell with Tottenham before ending his career in Japan.

JOSEF MASOPUST (born 9 February 1931)
Czechoslovakia: 63 games, 10 goals

Josef Masopust was the leading post-war heir to the great traditions of Czechoslovak football. An attacking midfielder, he played the majority of his career with the army club Dukla Prague before moving to Belgium and turning out for Crossing Molenbeek. He reached his peak at the 1962 World Cup in Chile, where he helped to inspire his side all the way to the final. Although he opened the scoring against Brazil, the holders fought back to triumph 3-1. Masopust won the 1962 Footballer of the Year award following his outstanding displays in Chile, where he was nicknamed "the Czech Knight."

SIR STANLEY MATTHEWS (born 1 February 1915, died 23 February 2000)
England: 54 games, 11 goals

Sir Stanley Matthews was the first active player to be knighted as reward for extraordinary service to the game both before and after World War II. He was an outside right whose mesmerizing talent earned him the nickname the "Wizard of Dribble." Matthews achieved his ambition to win the FA Cup with Blackpool in 1953, when, aged 38, he famously rescued his side from a 3-1 deficit by setting up three goals. In 1956, he received the

inaugural European Player of the Year award. His fitness and enthusiasm saw him play at the 1954 World Cup finals and then lead his original club, Stoke City, to promotion back into the old first division in 1962.

ABOVE Stanley Matthews teasing Manchester United's Roger Byrne in an international training session

GIUSEPPE MEAZZA (born 23 August 1910, died 21 August 1979)
Italy: 53 games, 33 goals

Giuseppe Meazza was one of only two Italian players—Giovanni Ferrari was the other—to have won the World Cup for the Azzurri both at home and also away. Meazza was a powerful, goalscoring inside forward with Internazionale in the 1930s, scoring 287 goals in 408 games for the club. He was a World Cup winner at home in 1934 and was the captain in France when Italy triumphed in 1938. He won three league titles and finished as top scorer in Serie A three times. He played briefly for AC Milan and guested for Juventus and Varese during World War II. He finished his playing career at Atalanta before managing Internazionale.

GREAT PLAYERS
EUROPEAN PLAYERS

BOBBY MOORE (born 12 April 1941, died 24 February 1993)
England: 108 games, 2 goals
Bobby Moore proved to be England's most successful captain, leading them to victory at the 1966 World Cup. He was skipper again during their unsuccessful defense of the trophy in 1970. He played for the majority of his career with West Ham United, initially as an attacking wing half before moving to the heart of defense. Respected by his team-mates for his tough tackling and silky skills, Moore achieved a remarkable hat-trick at Wembley Stadium by winning the FA Cup in 1964, the European Cup Winners' Cup in 1965, and the World Cup in 1966. A bronze statue of Moore stands outside the new Wembley. He finished his career with Fulham, San Antonio, and finally Seattle.

GERD MÜLLER (born 3 November 1945)
West Germany: 62 games, 68 goals
Gerd Müller was the most prolific goalscorer in modern football and, from 1974 to 2006, the all-time top scorer at the World Cup finals. He was voted European Player of the Year in 1970, having scored ten times at that year's World Cup finals in Mexico—he hit successive hat-tricks against Bulgaria and Peru—to finish as the highest scorer and win the Golden Boot. He notched an incredible 398 goals for Bayern Munich, where he was a key figure during the mid-1970s, when they won the European Cup three times in succession. He also scored the winning goal for West Germany in the 1974 World Cup final victory over Holland.

PAVEL NEDVED (born 30 August 1972)
Czech Republic: 91 games, 18 goals
The prolific Czech attacking midfielder was voted European Footballer of the Year in 2003. He might have achieved even more but for suspension and injury. He was banned for the 2003 European Champions League final, which Juventus lost to Milan on penalties. He was also injured early in the Euro 2004 semi-final when the Czechs lost to Greece on a "Silver Goal." Nedved started with Dukla Prague then made his name with Sparta. He starred in the Czech Republic side which reached the Euro '96 final. That earned him a move to Lazio whom he helped win the Italian title in 2000. He joined Juventus a year later and gained two title medals with them. He netted 18 goals in 91 appearances for his country.

FERENC PUSKÁS (born 2 April 1927, died 17 November 2006)
Hungary: 85 games, 84 goals; **Spain:** 4 games, no goals

BELOW Gerd Müller (right) shields the ball from Uruguayan defender Atilio Ancheta during the 1970 World Cup

game, he proved to be dangerous anywhere in attack and a real handful in the air. In the 2007–08 season, he scored 42 goals in all competitions, which propelled Manchester United to a double of the English league title and the Champions League. He gained Premier League title medals in 2007, 2008, and 2009. He was voted World Player of the Year in 2008.

WAYNE ROONEY (born 24 October 1985)
England: 67 games, 26 goals
The 16-year-old Rooney announced his arrival with a winning goal for Everton against champions Arsenal in October 2002. He then starred for England at Euro 2004 before injury forced him out of the quarter-final against Portugal. He made a $50 million (£28 m) move to Manchester United that summer. After the departure of Cristiano Ronaldo, he became United's star player. He was outstanding in the early part of the 2009–10 season, but an ankle injury took the edge off his

LEFT Ferenc Puskás, legendary No 10 for Honved and Real Madrid

BELOW Cristiano Ronaldo runs with the ball during a 2010 Real Madrid versus AC Milan Champions League match

Ferenc Puskás is one of the game's all-time greats, famed for his goals, his leadership, and the way that he rejuvenated his career after the 1956 Hungarian Revolution. Puskás and Hungary were unbeaten for four years, going into the 1954 World Cup finals as Olympic champions, but fell 3–2 to West Germany in the final. Puskás defected to the West, where he rebuilt his career with Real Madrid and won the league title five times and the European Cup three times.

CRISTIANO RONALDO (born 5 February 1985)
Portugal: 78 games, 25 goals
Cristiano Ronaldo became the world's most expensive player when he moved from Manchester United to Real Madrid for $132 million (£80 m) in the summer of 2009. United had paid more than $20 million (£12 m) for him in 2003. Once he adapted to the difficult demands of the English

Wayne Rooney (No 10) scores for England against Belarus in 2008 during a World Cup 2010 qualification match

EUROPEAN PLAYERS

game and he struggled in the 2010 World Cup finals. He helped United win the Premiership in 2007, 2008—when they also lifted the European Champions League—and 2009. Rooney was a League Cup winner in 2006 and 2010. He has scored 26 goals in 67 England appearances.

PAOLO ROSSI (born 23 September 1956)
Italy: 48 games, 20 goals
Paolo Rossi looked a great prospect after the 1978 World Cup finals, but he was banned for two years over a match-fixing scandal. The striker only returned to top-class action weeks before the 1982 World Cup finals kicked off, yet he finished as the top scorer with six goals to his credit. These strikes included a hat-trick to deliver the knock-out blow to Brazil in the quarter-final. Rossi continued to score, helping guide Italy to become world champions and himself to win the coveted Golden Boot.

MATTHIAS SINDELAR (born 10 February 1903, died 23 January 1939)
Austria: 43 games, 27 goals
Matthias Sindelar was the inspirational center forward of the Austrian "Wunderteam" that ruled European football in the late 1920s and early 1930s. Sindelar, nicknamed the "Man of Paper" because of his delicate build, won a league title, twice triumphed in the Mitropa Cup, and scored five Austrian Cup successes with Austria Vienna. A World Cup semi-finalist in 1934, he died of carbon monoxide poisoning in his Viennese apartment in unexplained circumstances five years later.

HRISTO STOICHKOV (born 8 February 1966)
Bulgaria: 83 games, 37 goals
Hristo Stoichkov, once banned for life from the sport but reinstated on appeal, was a huge success at club and national team level. In 1994, he picked up the European Player of the Year prize and won the Golden Boot as joint highest scorer at the World Cup finals as he inspired Bulgaria to reach the semi-finals. His move to Barcelona in 1990 saw him collect four Spanish league titles and the Spanish cup once.

FRITZ WALTER (born 31 October 1920, died 17 June 2002)
West Germany: 61 games, 33 goals
Fritz Walter owed his life to national manager Sepp Herberger and repaid him in glory. Walter, an inside forward from Kaiserslautern who made his international debut just before World War II, was kept away from the front by Herberger's string-pulling before finally being drafted in 1942.

He was captured and eventually repatriated by the Soviet army. He relaunched his football career and captained Herberger's West Germany to their unexpected World Cup final victory over favorites Hungary in 1954.

LEV YASHIN (born 22 October 1929, died 20 March 1990)

Soviet Union: 78 games, no goals

Lev Yashin, nicknamed the "Black Spider," ranks as arguably the greatest ever goalkeeper. Originally an ice hockey star, he succeeded "Tiger" Khomich between the posts at Dynamo Moscow in the early 1950s. Yashin won a gold medal in the 1956 Olympics, followed by victory at the 1960 European Championship. In 1963 he became the first goalkeeper to capture the European Player of the Year prize. Yashin played in three World Cup finals, reaching the semi-finals on his last appearance in 1966. He was awarded the Order of Lenin in 1967 and he retired in 1971. He is immortalized in the form of a statue at the entrance to the Dynamo Stadium in Moscow.

ZINEDINE ZIDANE (born June 23, 1972)

France: 108 games, 31 goals

Zidane was the outstanding French playmaker of the late 1990s and early 2000s. He was making headlines until the very last moment of his career—he was sent off in extra time in the 2006 World Cup final, his last game, for head butting Italy's Marco Materazzi. He scored twice in France's 1998 World Cup final win over Brazil and also starred for Bordeaux, Juventus, and Real Madrid.

DINO ZOFF (born 28 February 1942)

Italy: 112 games, no goals

Dino Zoff made his name with Udinese and Mantova before making the big time, first with Napoli and later with Juventus. He set numerous records at Juventus and picked up almost every title possible—initially as player and then as coach. Zoff was Italy's goalkeeper captain when they swept past all opponents at the 1982 World Cup finals. Aged 40, Zoff was the oldest player to win the World Cup after the Azzurri beat West Germany 3-1 in the final. After retiring as Italy's most capped player, he coached Juventus, Lazio, and Fiorentina, as well as the national team, which he guided to the final of the 2000 European Championship.

LEFT Captains Fritz Walter of West Germany (left) and Ferenc Puskás of Hungary (right) shaking hands prior to the start of the 1954 World Cup final

BELOW Dino Zoff saves against Brazil in the 1978 World Cup

1930s   1950s   1960s

ABOVE Dixie Dean runs out for Everton at the start of a league match against Arsenal

BELOW Raymond Kopa (left) playing for France in a 1952 friendly against Belgium

ABOVE Alfredo Di Stefano scores for Real Madrid against Eintracht

RIGHT Eusébio in training for a match against England

BELOW Bobby Charlton shoots for goal against France at Wembley

1970s

ABOVE Gerd Müller, triple European champion with Bayern Munich

BELOW Franz Beckenbauer (left) closes in on England's Colin Bell

ABOVE Sepp Maier in training in Munich's Olympic stadium

LEFT Franz Beckenbauer hoists aloft the World Cup in 1974

BELOW Uli Hoeness finds space in the World Cup final

AMERICAS PLAYERS

OSVALDO ARDILES (born 3 August 1952)
Argentina: 63 games, 8 goals

"Ossie" was the playmaker behind Argentina's World Cup win on home territory in 1978. The former Huracan midfielder played 63 times for his country. He was one of the first foreign players to succeed in England. He and compatriot Ricky Villa became cult figures at Tottenham. Ardiles spurred Tottenham to FA Cup final victory in 1981 but missed out the following season, because he joined Argentina's World Cup preparations before the FA Cup final. He was a second-leg substitute in the Spurs side that beat Anderlecht to win the UEFA Cup in 1984. He later managed in England, Mexico, Croatia, Japan, Argentina, and Paraguay. He was named Japan's Manager of the Year in 1998 for his success with Shimzu S-Pulse.

ANTONIO CARBAJAL (born 7 June 1929)
Mexico: 48 games, no goals

Antonio Carbajal became the first player to appear in the finals of five World Cup competitions, but ended up on the winning side only once. The Leon goalkeeper's debut in the finals was against Brazil in 1950, when he conceded four goals. He played in the 1954, 1958, and 1962 World Cup finals before bowing out after a scoreless draw against Uruguay in the 1966 group stages. Carbajal started at Club Espana in Mexico City, then joined Leon where he played the rest of his career.

JOSÉ LUIS CHILAVERT (born 27 July 1965)
Paraguay: 74 games, 8 goals

José Luis Chilavert was renowned for his scoring achievements despite being a goalkeeper. He claimed 62 goals from penalties and free kicks in a 22-year career with clubs in Argentina, France, Paraguay, Spain, and Uruguay (Spain was the only country where he did not win at least one league title.) Chilavert's ultimate ambition was to score a goal in the World Cup finals, but he failed, despite having netted four in qualifying matches for the 2002 tournament. He was voted South America's Footballer of the Year in 1996.

ROBERTO CARLOS (born 10 April 1973)
Brazil: 125 games, 11 goals

Roberto Carlos da Silva Rocha proved to be one of Brazil's most popular exports to Europe because of his thunderous shooting and his exuberant attacking play from left back. In 2002,

RIGHT Roberto Carlos clears the ball for Real Madrid during a 2006 Champions League match against Olympique Lyonnais

he won the World Cup with Brazil and the European Cup with Real Madrid. Roberto Carlos played more games for Real Madrid than any other foreigner, before moving to Turkey with Fenerbahce. He later returned to Brazil with Corinthians.

TEÓFILO CUBILLAS (born 8 March 1949)
Peru: 81 games, 26 goals

Teófilo Cubillas shot to stardom as an inside forward in the Peru team that reached the 1970 World Cup quarter-finals and the second round at the 1978 World Cup finals. Cubillas was voted South American Player of the Year in 1972, and won the Copa America with Peru in 1975. He began his career with Alianza of Lima, then played in Switzerland, Portugal, and the United States.

DIDI (born 8 October 1929, died 12 May 2001)
Brazil: 68 games, 20 goals

Didi, full name Valdir Pereira, won the World Cup twice with Brazil in 1958 and 1962. Brazil might not have even been at the finals in 1958 at all, but for a remarkable free kick from Didi that bent in the air and flew into the net against Peru in a qualifying tie. The "Falling Leaf" became Didi's trademark and has been copied by players all over the world ever since. He played most of his career with Botafogo of Rio de Janeiro either side of a short, unhappy spell in 1959–60 with Real Madrid.

ALFREDO DI STEFANO (born 4 July 1926)
Argentina: 6 games, 6 goals; **Spain:** 31 games, 23 goals

Alfredo Di Stefano remains, for many experts, the greatest ever player because of his all-action performances as a pitch-roaming, high-scoring center forward. He starred for Argentina's River Plate and Colombia's Millonarios, before inspiring Real Madrid to victory in the first five European Cup competitions. Di Stefano scored in all five finals, and totaled 216 league goals for Real Madrid over 11 years.

LANDON DONOVAN (born 4 March 1982)
United States: 128 games, 45 goals

Landon Donovan has proved himself one of US football's greatest servants. By the age of 26 the midfielder had already reached a century of international appearances and played at two World Cup finals. Donovan began at German club Bayer Leverkusen before returning to the US with San Jose Earthquakes, then joining LA Galaxy. He went on loan to Bayern Munich in 2009, and had a loan spell with Premier League club Everton a year later.

ENZO FRANCESCOLI (born 12 November 1961)
Uruguay: 72 games, 15 goals

Enzo Francescoli, nicknamed "The Prince," is arguably the last great Uruguayan player. However, he played the majority of his club career in Argentina, France, and Italy. He played the 1989–90 season with Olympique Marseille, where he was the footballing hero and inspiration for the teenage Zinedine Zidane. A tall, graceful inside forward, Francescoli was a three-times winner of the Copa America with Uruguay and played twice at the World Cup finals. He was voted South American Player of the Year in both 1984 and 1995.

ABOVE Alfredo Di Stefano scores for Real Madrid against Manchester United

AMERICAS PLAYERS

GARRINCHA (born 28 October 1933, died 20 January 1983)
Brazil: 50 games, 12 goals
Garrincha, full name Manoel dos Santos Francisco, lived a life that was a tale of triumph and tragedy. Nicknamed "the Little Bird," he won the World Cup in 1958 and 1962, with his goals proving to be decisive. He was at Rio's Botafogo for 12 years, scoring 232 goals in 581 games. Yet his love of the good life meant he was also his own worst enemy and a nightmare for coaches. He tragically died of alcohol poisoning.

GÉRSON (born 11 January 1941)
Brazil: 70 games, 14 goals
Gérson de Oliveira Nunes was the strolling playmaker of Brazil's great 1970 World Cup winning team. He was one of the game's great long passers, with a deadly accurate left foot. He could score memorable goals too, such as the 25-yarder which restored Brazil's lead in the World Cup final against Italy. He netted 14 in 70 games for his country. The 1970 tournament was the highlight of his career. He graduated through Brazil's 1960 Olympic side but missed the 1962 World Cup win because of a knee injury and played only once in 1966. Gérson began his club career with Flamengo, then moved to Rio rivals Botafogo, where he won the Brazilian championship forerunner in 1968. He later played for São Paulo and Fluminense.

JAIRZINHO (born 25 December 1944)
Brazil: 81 games, 33 goals
Jairzinho, full name Jair Ventura Filho, was the free-scoring successor to the Brazilian tradition of great outside rights, from Julinho in the mid-1950s to Garrincha in the late 1950s and 1960s. He played, like his hero Garrincha, for Rio's Botafogo. In 1970, he recovered twice from a broken right leg and became the only player to score in every round of the World Cup finals in Mexico, netting seven goals overall. Jairzinho, nicknamed "God," also played in the World Cup finals of 1966 and 1974. He famously discovered an outstanding 12-year-old in Rio de Janeiro, a talent called Ronaldo.

KAKÁ (born 22 April 1982)
Brazil: 82 games, 27 goals
Kaká, full name Ricardo Izecson dos Santos Leite, was generally hailed as the world's top player in 2007, when he set up AC Milan's European Champions League victory and was voted World Player of the Year and European Player of the Year. The gifted Brazilian forward originally made his name with São Paulo, following a remarkable recovery from a swimming pool accident that left him temporarily paralyzed. AC Milan paid a comparatively low $10 million (£6 m) for him in 2003. He moved to Real Madrid in a $93 million (£55 m) deal in the summer of 2009.

LUCIO (born 8 May 1978)
Brazil: 96 games, 5 goals
Lucimar Ferreira da Silva is one of Brazil's best-ever defenders—and a star of Internazionale's 2010 European Champions League success. The powerful center back was the defensive linchpin of the Brazil side which won the 2002 World Cup. He appeared again in the 2006 and 2010 campaigns which both ended in the quarter-finals. Lucio began his club career with Internacional of Porto Alegre. He later reached the 2002 European Champions League final with Bayer Leverkusen and won three Bundesliga titles with Bayern Munich. He joined Inter in the summer of 2009, helped them win the Italian title for the 18th time, then starred in defense as they beat Bayern 2-0 in the 2010 European Champions League final.

MARIO KEMPES (born 15 July 1954)
Argentina: 43 games, 20 goals

Mario Kempes emerged with Rosario Central in the early 1970s and was one of the finest prospects on view when he played for Argentina at the 1974 World Cup finals. Valencia snapped up Kempes, who twice finished leading scorer in Spain and was one of only two foreign-based players called up by Argentina boss César Luis Menotti for the 1978 World Cup. Kempes was an inspiration, scoring six goals for the hosts, including two in the extra time final victory over Holland.

DIEGO MARADONA (born 30 October 1960)
Argentina: 91 games, 34 goals

Diego Maradona ranks among the greatest ever players, despite off-field controversy and the "Hand of God" goal against England in the 1986 World Cup quarter-finals. Discovered by Argentinos Juniors, he starred for Boca Juniors before moving for world record fees to Barcelona and then Napoli. Captain and inspiration in the 1986 World Cup finals, his second strike against England is considered to be one of the greatest ever goals. A runner-up in the 1990 World Cup, he was suspended in 1991 after failing a drugs test, and three years later failed a World Cup finals doping

test. He was appointed Argentina coach in 2008, despite a lack of coaching experience, and guided them to the 2010 World Cup quarter-finals.

LIONEL MESSI (born 24 June 1987)
Argentina: 53 games, 15 goals

Messi is one of the superstars of the modern era. He left Rosario, Argentina at 13 in 2000 for Barcelona, who arranged growth hormone treatment to build him up. He is small, quick, a brilliant dribbler and a deadly finisher. He made his name with six goals in the World Youth Cup in 2005. He won an Olympic gold for Argentina in 2006—the season he broke through at Barcelona, netting a hat-trick against Real Madrid. He has played in four Barcelona title-winning teams, helped settle their King's Cup success in 2009 and headed the decisive second goal against Manchester United in the European Champions League final. He was named FIFA World Player of the Year and European Player of the Year in 2009.

PELÉ (born 23 October 1940)
Brazil: 92 games, 77 goals

Pelé, full name Edson Arantes do Nascimento, made his league debut for Santos aged 15. One of only a few who could realistically claim to be the greatest footballer who ever played, he was a World Cup winner at 17—scoring twice in the 5-2 victory over Sweden in the 1958 final. Injury prevented Pelé playing in the 1962 World Cup final and he endured an unhappy tournament in 1966, but he was back at his best for the 1970 final and scored in the 4-1 win over Italy. He came out of retirement in 1975 to help New York Cosmos spearhead the North American Soccer League revolution before hanging up his boots in 1977, having amassed more than 1,000 goals.

LEFT Argentina captain Diego Maradona had a big hand in winning the 1986 World Cup

BELOW Bobby Moore with Pelé at the 1970 World Cup

Kaká (left) dribbles past Yaya Toure and Siaka Tiene during the Brazil versus Ivory Coast group match at the 2010 World Cup

GREAT PLAYERS
AMERICAS PLAYERS

ABOVE Hugo Sánchez leaps off the pitch as he attempts to take control of the ball in a 1986 World Cup match

ROBERTO RIVELINO (born 1 January 1946)
Brazil: 92 games, 26 goals

Rivelino was the moustachioed dead ball expert of Brazil's 1970 World Cup winners. He cracked a thunderous free kick to level in the opening game against Czechoslovakia which earned him the nickname "Atomic Shot." He netted again in the quarter-final against Peru and the semi-final against Uruguay. Rivelino was a gifted creative midfielder, noted for his passing, over five yards or 50. He was one of the few Brazilians to emerge with credit from their unsuccessful World Cup campaign four years later. He scored 26 goals in 92 games for his country. He spent nearly 10 years at Corinthians in São Paulo—where he was nicknamed "King of the Park"—then helped Fluminense win two Rio de Janeiro championships in the mid-1970s.

RONALDINHO (born 21 March 1980)
Brazil: 87 games, 32 goals

Ronaldinho, full name Ronaldo de Assis Moreira, was the attacking midfielder who inspired Barcelona to two league titles and also victory in the 2006 Champions League. He joined Barcelona after spells with Grêmio in Brazil and Paris Saint-Germain. A key figure in Brazil's 2002 World Cup win, Ronaldinho was voted World Player of the Year in 2004 and 2005. He moved to AC Milan in 2008.

RONALDO (born 22 September 1976)
Brazil: 97 games, 62 goals

Ronaldo Luis Nazário de Lima was discovered as a 12-year-old by World Cup-winner Jairzinho. Five years later, he was at the 1994 World Cup, albeit a non-playing member of the Brazilian squad. In 1998, he was a runner-up amid controversy—playing despite having been taken ill shortly before Brazil's final defeat by France. Ronaldo made amends by scoring twice in the 2002 World Cup final win over Germany and netted a record 15th World Cup goal at the 2006 finals. Knee injuries have marred much of his career with PSV Eindoven, Barcelona, Internazionale, Real Madrid, and AC Milan. He returned to Brazil with Corinthians in 2009.

HUGO SÁNCHEZ (born 11 July 1958)
Mexico: 58 games, 29 goals

Hugo Sánchez numbers among the most prolific scorers in the history of Mexican football and as one of its greatest personalities. He led the attack in three World Cup finals, and ranks as the second-highest overall scorer in Spain's La Liga, with 234 goals amassed at Atletico Madrid and Real Madrid. He was the international manager of Mexico for 16 months until March 2008.

HÉCTOR SCARONE (born 1 January 1900, died 4 April 1967)
Uruguay: 51 games, 31 goals

Héctor Scarone, nicknamed "the Magician," was the original star of the World Cup after leading Uruguay to victory over Argentina in the inaugural finals in 1930. He played briefly in Europe with Barcelona and Internazionale, and for two seasons with Palermo. He won eight Uruguayan league titles and scored 301 goals in 369 games with Nacional Montevideo.

PEDRO ALBERTO SPENCER (born 6 December 1937, died 3 November 2006)
Ecuador: 11 games, 4 goals;
Uruguay: 4 games, 1 goal

Pedro Spencer is record scorer in the history of

the Copa Libertadores. He netted 54 goals in 12 years, mostly for Uruguay's Peñarol, and was the first world-famous Ecuadorian player. Spencer had been recommended to Peñarol—with whom he went on to win two Club World Cups and eight league titles—by Juan Lopez, Uruguay's manager for the 1950 World Cup win in Brazil.

CARLOS VALDERRAMA (born 2 September 1961)
Colombia: 111 games, 11 goals
Carlos Valderrama, nicknamed "The Kid," was a colorful midfielder who led Colombia at the World Cup finals of 1990, 1994, and 1998. He was renowned almost as much for his outrageous, long blond hair as for his supreme talent. He was voted South American Player of the Year in 1987 and 1993 and represented Colombia a record 111 times. He spent most of his 22-year career in Colombia, although he played for Montpellier in France and Real Valladolid in Spain before a six-year career in the United States MLS.

OBDULIO VARELA (born 20 September 1917, died 2 August 1996)
Uruguay: 49 games, 10 goals
Obdulio Varela was the attacking center half who captained Uruguay to World Cup victory in 1950. Varela apparently told the team to ignore their manager's talk and follow his orders—they bounced back with two goals to spring one of the World Cup's greatest shocks: a 2-1 win over Brazil.

IVAN ZAMORANO (born 18 January 1967)
Chile: 69 games, 34 goals
Ivan Zamorano was Chile's iconic hero in the 1990s, when he led the national team's World Cup attack and starred in European football. Zamorano was brought to Europe by the Swiss club Saint Gallen. After three terms he moved to Spain for six seasons. In 1995 he was the league's top scorer,

with 27 goals for Real Madrid. He went on to win the 1998 UEFA Cup with Internazionale before returning to Chile with Colo Colo via a two-year stint in Mexico.

ZICO (born 3 March 1953)
Brazil: 88 games, 66 goals
Zico, full name Artur Antunes Coimbra, shot to stardom with Rio de Janerio's Flamengo in the mid-1970s. He followed his 16-year career in Brazil with a two-year spell with Udinese in Italy before returning to Flamengo. However, despite being a legendary Brazil forward, he failed to win a World Cup and missed a crucial World Cup quarter-final penalty against France in 1986. He won the 1990 Club World Cup, inspiring Flamengo's victory over Liverpool. He coached in Japan, Turkey, Uzbekistan, Russia, and Greece, then returned to Flamengo in May 2010, for a four-month stint as technical director.

BELOW Zico takes on Argentina's Jorge Olguin in the 1982 World Cup finals

1980s

1990s

ABOVE France winger Didier Six (right) takes on the Czech defense

BELOW Ossie Ardiles in English action for Tottenham

ABOVE Carlos Valderrama (left) in action for Colombia at the 1998 World Cup

LEFT Ivan Zamorano (right) celebrates a Marcelo Salas (left) goal at the 1998 World Cup

ABOVE Eric Cantona making his debut for Manchester United

2000s

ABOVE Lionel Messi celebrates scoring for Argentina against France in a 2009 friendly match

BELOW Cristiano Ronaldo top-scored with 31 goals in the 2008 Premier League

ABOVE David Beckham strikes a winning penalty against Argentina

LEFT Steven Gerrard celebrates another of his England goals

BELOW Ronaldinho in action for Barcelona against Bayern Munich

BELOW Samuel Eto'o (right) evades Bastian Schweinsteiger (left) during the 2010 Champions League final

GREAT PLAYERS
REST OF THE WORLD

ABOVE Hong Myung-Bo is challenged by Mexican forward Cuauhtemoc Blanco in 1998

DIDIER DROGBA (born 11 March 1978)
Ivory Coast: 71 games, 45 goals
Didier Drogba was a late starter, not making his professional breakthrough until he was 20 with French club Le Mans. He moved on to Guingamp at the age of 24 before being bought by Marseille, whom he led to the 2004 UEFA Cup final. His next step was a transfer to newly-enriched Chelsea, for a then club record $48 million (£24 m). He has scored more than 100 goals for them and finished Premier League top scorer in 2010. He has won the Premier League (three times), FA Cup (three times), and League Cup (twice). Drogba was named African Player of the Year in 2007 and 2009.

SAMUEL ETO'O (born 10 March 1981)
Cameroon: 101 games, 52 goals
Explosive striker Samuel Eto'o gained three

European Champions League winner's medals in five seasons—with Barcelona in 2006 and 2009, then with Internazionale in 2010. He scored the equalizer in Barcelona's 2-1 win over Arsenal and the opening goal in their 2-0 victory against Manchester United in 2009. He joined Inter that summer, in a swap deal involving Zlatan Ibrahimovic. In 2006, Eto'o also won the Golden Boot as Europe's leading league scorer. He is the all-time top scorer in the African Nations Cup finals.

HONG MYUNG-BO (born 12 February 1969)
South Korea: 135 games, 9 goals
Hong Myung-Bo was the first Asian player to appear in four World Cup finals tournaments. Originally a powerful defensive midfielder, he was soon switched to central defense. He made his international debut in 1990 and was chosen to be part of the South Korean World Cup squad in Italy later that year. He earned international admiration for his displays in the 1994 and 1998 World Cup finals, despite his side's first round exits. He was a national hero long before he captained South Korea to the last four on home territory at the 2002 World Cup finals.

HOSSAM HASSAN (born 10 August 1966)
Egypt: 169 games, 69 goals
Hossam Hassan is one of the world's most capped players with 169 appearances for the Pharaohs. His Egypt record was only surpassed in 2010 by current skipper Ahmed Hassan. He retired as a player in 2007 after setting a host of Egyptian records. He won 41 titles, played 21 matches over seven African Nations Cup competitions, and was

the oldest scorer in an Egypt shirt. Hossam has also played for Paok Saloniki in Greece, Neuchatel Xamax in Switzerland, and El-Ain in the UAE. He was appointed coach of Egyptian giants Zamalek at the end of 2009.

ROGER MILLA (born 20 May 1952)
Cameroon: 102 games, 28 goals

Roger Milla had long been an African hero before his celebration dance around the corner flags brought him global fame at the 1990 World Cup. Milla scored four times at those finals, making him the oldest ever World Cup scorer at the age of 38. He returned to the World Cup finals four years later, before retiring with an impressive record. He twice picked up the African Player of the Year award (1976 and 1990), and in 2007 was voted the best African Player of the last 50 years in a Confederation of African Football (CAF) poll.

HIDETOSHI NAKATA (born 22 January 1977)
Japan: 77 games, 11 goals

Hidetoshi Nakata was the first Japanese player to make a major impact in Europe. Nakata, the Asian Player of the Year in 1997 and 1998, moved to Italy after his World Cup finals debut at France 98. He played in the next two World Cup finals, announcing his shock retirement immediately after the 2006 World Cup match against Brazil in Germany. Nakata played seven seasons for various sides in Italy's Serie A and had a short spell in England's Premier League with Bolton Wanderers.

JAY-JAY OKOCHA (born 14 August 1973)
Nigeria: 74 games, 14 goals

Augustine "Jay-Jay" Okocha provided the midfield command that lifted Nigeria's "Super Eagles" out of the also-rans of Africa to regular appearances at the World Cup finals. He played in the 1994, 1998, and 2002 finals, but the "Super Eagles" failed to qualify for the 2006 finals. Okocha also helped Nigeria win the 1996 Olympic gold medal, yet never won an African Player of the Year award. He played for a variety of clubs in Germany, Turkey, France, and England. At the end of the 2007–08 season, after helping Hull City attain Premier League status, he was released from his contract and retired.

SAEED AL-OWAIRAN (born 19 August 1967)
Saudi Arabia: 50 games, 24 goals

Saeed Al-Owairan won the accolade of the Asian Player of the Year in 1994, largely thanks to his memorable solo strike against Belgium in that year's World Cup finals. His goal for Saudi Arabia was comparable with Diego Maradona's sensational strike against England in 1986. Al-Owairan had only played as a professional for two years before his famous goal.

LEFT Samuel Eto'o celebrates yet another goal for Barcelona in 2008

ABOVE Roger Milla's World Cup exploits earned him a string of international awards

Didier Drogba (left) challenges Gilberto Silva (right) during the Ivory Coast versus Brazil group match at the 2010 World Cup

PICTURE
CREDITS

The publisher would like to thank the following for permission to reproduce the following copyright material:

Key: t: top, c: center, b: bottom, l: left, r: right

Front Cover image: Getty Images

Endpapers: Istock.

Corbis: 7 Hulton-Deutsch Collection, 8 Bettmann, 18/19 Bettmann, 22/23 Bettmann, 27/27 dpa, 37 (tr) Oliver Berg/dpa, 37 (c) Oliver Multhaup/dpa, 37 (bl) Andrew Cowie/Colorsport, 43/42 Tim De Waele, 47 (t) Georgi Licovski/epa, 47 (b) Matthew Ashton/AMA, 48/49 Eva-Lotta Jansson, 50 (tr) Tim De Waele, 50 (c) Matthias Schrader/dpa, 50 (bl) P. Caron/Corbis Sygma, 51 (tr) Paul Zammit Cutajar/Colorsport, 51 (cr) Andres Kudacki, 51 (bl) Oliver Berg/dpa, 51 (br) Helmut Fohringer/epa, 60/61 Gilbert Iundt/TempSport, 68/69 Liao Yujie/Xinhua Press, 70 Radek Pietruszka/epa, 71 Ben Radford, 72 Bogdan Borowiak/epa, 73 Grzegorz Michalowski/epa, 74 Adam Ciereszko/epa, 75 Ettore Ferrari/epa, 82/83 Neil Marchand/Liewig Media Sports, 88/89 Ali Haider/epa, 108/109 Ben Radford, 126/127 Sampics, 134/135 Toby Melville/Reuters, 144/145 Eva-Lotta Jansson, 166/167 Kerim Okten/epa, 177 Marcus Brandt/epa, 18 (t) Schirner Sportfoto Archiv/dpa, 182/183 Catherine Ivill/AMA/, 185 (t) Vassil Donev/epa, 186 (tr and br) Bettman, 188 Matthew Ashton/AMA, 191 Stephane Mantey/TempSport, 192/193 Stephane Mantey/TempSport, 196 Jean-Yves Ruszniewski/TempSport, 198/199 Helmut Fohringer/epa, 202 Heidtmann/dpa, 203 (b) Andres Kudacki, 204/205 Matthew Ashton/AMA, 206 Melchert/dpa, 207 (t) epa, 208 (tl and cr) Hulton-Deutsch Collection, 208 (bl) Universal/TempSport, 210 Stephane Reix/For Picture, 212 Universal/TempSport, 214/215 Joe Toth/BPI, 216 Bettman, 218 (tl) Franck Seguin/TempSport, 218 (c) Thierry Orban, 219 (tl) Ben Radford, 219 (bl) Alberto Martin/epa, 219 (br) Christian Liewig/Liewig Media Sports, 222/223 Kerim Okten/epa.

Mirrorpix: 21, 28 (tl, tr, and br), 29 (tl, tc, c, bl, tr, br), 36 (tl, c, bl, tr, and br), 37 (tl, br), 62 (c, tr), 63 (tl, bc, br), 90 (tl, bl, tr, br), 91 (tl, bl, c, br), 95, 102 (b, tr, cr), 103 (tl, cl, tr,), 120, 121, 125 (l and r), 129, 130 (tl, bl, c, tr, br), 131 (tl, bl, c, tr, br), 132, 139, 141, 152, 155, 157, 160, 163, 168 (tr, br,), 169 (tr), 173, 178, 181 (b), 184, 186 (cr), 187 (tl), 190, 194, 200, 201, 203 (t), 207 (b), 208 (tr and br), 209, 213 (b), 217, 218 (tl, bl, br), 219 (tr, c, cl), 221 (r).

Getty Images: 2,3, 6, 9, 10, 12, 13, 14, 15, 16, 17, 20, 24, 25, 28 (c and bl), 30, 31, 33, 34, 35, 38, 39, 40, 41 (t and b), 45 (t and b), 50 (tl and br), 51 (tl), 52, 55 (t and b), 56, 57, 58, 59, 62 (tl, bl ,br), 63 (bl, tc, tr,), 65, 66, 67, 76, 77, 78, 79, 80 (t and b), 81, 84, 85, 86, 87, 90 (c), 91 (tr), 92, 93, 94 (l and r), 97 (t and b), 98, 99, 100, 101, 102 (tl, cl,), 103 (bl, cr, br), 104, 105, 106, 107 (l and r), 110, 111, 112 (tl, bl, c, tr, br), 113 (tl, bl, tc, c, tr, br), 114, 115, 147 (t and b), 118, 119, 122, 123, 124, 131 (cr), 133, 136, 137, 140, 142, 143, 146, 147, 148, 149, 150, 151, 153, 154, 156, 158, 159, 161, 162, 164, 165, 168 (tl, bl, c),169 (tl, bl, tc, ,tr, cr, br), 170, 171, 172, 174, 175, 176, 179 (t and b), 180, 185 (b), 186 (tl and bl), 187 (cl, tc, tr, cr, b), 189, 195, 197, 211, 213 (t), 220, 221 (l).

Istock: 4, 5.

Every effort has been made to obtain permission to reproduce copyright material, but there may be cases where we have been unable to trace a copyright holder. The publisher will be happy to correct any omissions in future printings.